THE LEARNING SUPPORT TEACHER
A PRACTICAL HANDBOOK

©Thérèse McPhillips

FOR LEARNING SUPPORT TEACHERS, RESOURCE TEACHERS, CLASS TEACHERS, PARENTS, AND ANYONE INVOLVED IN HELPING THE CHILD WITH LEARNING DIFFICULTIES

Blackrock Education Centre
Ionad Oideachais na Carraige Duibhe

BLACKROCK EDUCATION CENTRE

First published 2003

by

Blackrock Education Centre

Kill Avenue

Dún Laoghaire

Co. Dublin

Telephone: (01) 236 5000

Email: bec@blackrock-edu.ie

Website: www.blackrock-edu.ie

Editor & Publishing Consultant: Roberta Reeners

Design by Design Image

Printed in Ireland by Criterion Press

CONTENTS

ACKNOWLEDGMENTS

The author wishes to acknowledge all those who contributed to the organisation, coordination and presentation of the Summer Inservice course, "The Learning Support Teacher: Practical Strategies", organised by Blackrock Education Centre and held in St Oliver Plunkett School, Monkstown, over the past three years. I am grateful to the many individuals who presented a session on the course during that time: Bríd Clancy, Aoife Byrne, Abigail Whyte, Mary Scullion, Chris Chapple, Angela Power, Brendan Culligan, Ann Jackson, Ursula Hearne, Christine Caplice and Mairead Dempsey.

I am especially grateful to Bríd Clancy, Aoife Byrne and Ann Jackson for their valuable contributions to this publication. Sincere thanks to Patricia Lynch and Brendan Culligan for editorial assistance. My thanks to my editor, Roberta Reeners, who guided me through the writing process with patience and good humour.

In particular, I wish to thank the Director of Blackrock Education Centre, Seamus Ó Canainn, for his support and encouragement in completing this Teacher's Manual. Special thanks to Evelyn Logan who typed the initial drafts, and to all the staff at the Centre — Lil Lynch, Tomás Ó Briain, Jenny Masterson, Róisín Phillips, Geraldine Byrne, Val Collins, Phil Halpin, Mary Sorohan, Siobhán Cluskey, Helen MacGoey, Tom MacMahon, Emer Bradley, Chris Murphy, Monica Dowdall, Aileen Benson, Ben O'Toole, Deborah Mooney, Heather Friel and Adela Fernandez.

I would also like to thank the Board of Management and the Teachers at St Oliver Plunkett School, Monkstown.

Finally, a sincere thank you to my husband and family for their support and encouragement.

The author and publisher wish to thank the following for permission to use copyright material: Aoife Byrne, East Coast Area Health Board; Mary Scullion, Lucena Clinic; Abigail White, Lucena Clinic; Bríd Clancy, National Educational Psychological Service; Ann Jackson, Central Remedial Clinic, Clontarf.
Every effort has been made to trace copyright holders and to acknowledge them accordingly. However, if any have been omitted inadvertently, correct acknowledgment will be made at the earliest opportunity.

THE AUTHOR

Thérèse McPhillips is Principal of St Oliver Plunkett Special School, Monkstown, Dublin, and a member of the Management Committee of Blackrock Education Centre. With over twenty years' experience teaching in mainstream and special schools, for the past three years, she has coordinated and presented a summer inservice course for Learning Support and Resource teachers, organised by Blackrock Education Centre. With an interest in special education, she was a member of the recent government Task Force on Dyslexia and is the coordinator of a European Comenius project. At present, Thérèse is undertaking PhD research at TCD in the area of dyslexia.

THE CONTRIBUTORS

Aoife Byrne is Principal Speech and Language Therapist in the East Coast Area Health Board, Loughlinstown, Co. Dublin. She is involved in providing a service to schools and families in the community care area of South Dublin. As part of her work, she frequently contributes to schools' inservice courses and consults with teachers regarding referral for Speech and Language therapy.

Bríd Clancy is an Educational Psychologist working with the National Educational Psychological Service. She is also a qualified teacher with experience in mainstream and special schools. As part of her work, Bríd contributes to inservice courses for Learning Support and Resource teachers. Over the past three summers, she has contributed to inservice courses for Learning Support and Resource teachers organised and coordinated by Blackrock Education Centre.

Ann Jackson is the National Technology and Special Needs Advisor. Appointed by the Department of Education and based in the Central Remedial Clinic in Clontarf, she provides advice and specialist training to teachers and other educationalists on the use of technology, particularly computers, in the education of students with special needs. Her seminars and presentations are aimed at making educationalists aware of the range of software and equipment available, where it can be sourced and, most importantly, the criteria for choosing appropriate and useful technology for individuals and groups of students. She can be contacted by voice mail at (01) 805 7545 but preferably by e-mail at ajackson@crc.ie.

Abigail White, Senior Clinical Psychologist, and **Mary Scullion**, Senior Speech and Language Therapist, the Lucena Clinic, Dun Laoghaire, have collaborated with Aoife Byrne on inservice presentations to Learning Support Teachers.

INTRODUCTION

This Teachers' Manual has been compiled to help the Learning Support Teacher (LST) to:

▸▸ *Recognise* the problems presented by children with Specific Learning Disabilities (SLDs).

▸▸ *Analyse* the extent of the problem(s).

▸▸ Begin to *organise* remediation.

The manual is a compilation of the teaching materials and resources which were developed over three years from summer inservice courses, "The Learning Support Teacher: Practical Strategies and Suggestions". The courses were organised by Blackrock Education Centre, whose objective it is to coordinate and provide inservice training in specific areas identified by teachers. These courses were designed to support the work of LSTs, especially those recently appointed to the position.

The teachers who attended these courses were interested in developing teaching skills and strategies which would meet the needs of children receiving learning support, particularly those children with Specific Learning Disabilities. Topics chosen for inclusion in the course were those which the author considered to be most important and relevant to the role of the LST.

In recent years, the term "Learning Support Teacher" has replaced "Remedial Teacher". In keeping with practice in England and United States, the term "learning support" is seen as a more positive description for the role of the teacher who assists the child who has difficulties with learning.

A LITERACY PROBLEM

Recent reports point to low levels of literacy among a proportion of primary and post-primary pupils. An article in the *Irish Journal of Education* (Martin & Morgan, 1994) stated that between 6.5% and 8.5% of Irish 14-year-olds were judged to have literacy problems which were likely to impede their educational development and their life chances. A Government White Paper on Education (1995) expressed the view that a significant minority do not acquire satisfactory levels of literacy and numeracy while at primary school. The National Assessment of English Reading in Fifth Class (Cosgrove, Kellaghan, Forde & Morgan 1998) showed that 11% of boys and 7% girls were judged by their teachers to be reading at third class level or lower.

The *Report of the Special Education Review Committee* (*SERC Report*, 1993) stated that 0.3% of the school-going population were already identified as having Specific Learning Disabilities. This is most likely an underestimate of the prevalence of the problem. Estimates in the literature vary between 2% and 4% of pupils in their age cohort with SLDs. A large number of undiagnosed dyslexic-type learning difficulties are included in these figures, as evidenced by submissions contained in the Report of the Task Force on Dyslexia (2002) and the Dyslexia Association of Ireland Survey (2002). According to the *OECD Report on Literacy* (2000), 20% of the Irish population are functioning at or below "Level 1".

In the light of research regarding standards of literacy among our primary school pupils, there is an urgency to recognise and identify those pupils who are underachieving in the areas of literacy and numeracy, whatever the reason.

CURRENT PROVISION IN IRELAND

While the attainment levels of some children will be at a level below the norm, their attainment will match their general ability level. The class teacher will notice and adjust his/her teaching accordingly. Other children will have a noticeable discrepancy between their ability level and their attainment in specific areas such as writing, reading or spelling. A psychological assessment is necessary to document and support the evidence of a Specific Learning Disability.

There are four main types of provision in Ireland for children with SLDs:

▸▸ **Assisted mainstream**: The child remains in ordinary class, with support from the Learning Support Teacher (LST).

▸▸ **Resource teaching**: The child with SLD may be assisted by a Resource Teacher. Generally, this involves withdrawing the child from his/her mainstream class and providing extra teaching on a 1-to-1 basis. Support may be continued for the length of the child's stay in primary school.

▸▸ **Special reading class**: This is a support unit in designated schools. There are 18 such classes around the country. The pupil-teacher ratio is 11:1. A temporary placement for up to two years is possible. Pupils are integrated with mainstream classes for some subjects such as history, geography, art, music etc.

▸▸ **Special Schools**: Some children attend special schools for pupils with SLDs. There are three such schools in Dublin and one in Cork. The total number enrolled is 250. Placement is for a maximum two years. All subjects are taught, but the emphasis throughout the day is on literacy skills.

POLICY DEVELOPMENTS IN REMEDIAL EDUCATION IN PRIMARY SCHOOLS 1988–2000

A summary look at previous guidelines on remedial education shows the direction of policy developments during these years.

NOTHING NEW!

The *Guidelines on Remedial Education* (Department of Education, 1988) recommended a *whole school approach* to remedial education in schools — a team approach with the remedial teacher in a consultative role. The latest guidelines (2000) repeat this recommendation, along with "whole school policies" and partnership and support for parents. The 1988 guidelines also recommended a *preventative* approach by targeting the junior classes. This is echoed in the new *guidelines* by the focus on early intervention programmes for pupils in senior infants to second class.

The *Report of the Special Education Review Committee* (Ireland, 1993) recommended expansion of the remedial service to all pupils who are at or below the 10th percentile. The latest guidelines (2000) suggest that pupils at or below the 10th percentile should have first priority for learning support.

A study of remedial education in Irish primary schools (Shiel, Morgan & Larney, 1998) suggested that "particular attention should be given to the appropriate use of cut-off scores in selecting pupils for remedial classes and in clarifying the concept of 'potential to benefit from remedial teaching'." (p. 42) In other words, the help and support a child receives should be related to his/her individual needs.

The *Report of the Task Force on Dyslexia* (2002) also underlines the importance of an individualised assessment and provision of support according to the level of that need.

The *Learning Support Guidelines* (Department of Education and Science/DES, 2000) propose that the LST develop and implement an "Individual Learning Programme" based on an individual assessment of need and setting learning targets for the pupil. (Further details of this proposal are outlined in another section of this manual.)

Principles Underpinning the Information in this Manual

The following personal views are central to the underlying rationale of this manual. These viewpoints are developed in each chapter and are supported by recent research and government publications.

▶▶ **Multidisciplinary team:** The LST does not operate in a vacuum. S/He is not solely responsible for individual pupils' needs. Collaboration with the class teacher, school principal, parents and other specialists such as the educational psychologist, speech therapist, occupational therapist etc. is essential to programme planning. Shared responsibility means shared involvement in programme planning, implementation and evaluation.

▶▶ **Principle of individual difference**: No two children with dyslexic-type reading difficulties (or any other SLD) will present with exactly the same profile. Each child's strengths and needs will be as individual as the child. Individualised assessment is central to effective intervention. The *Task Force Report on Dyslexia* favours "individualisation of provision to be an educational imperative and a legal requirement" (p. 15).

▶▶ **Diagnostic assessment:** When a child has been identified as achieving below a certain level, further testing is required to analyse the extent of her/his difficulties. This is known as *diagnostic assessment*. The LST is responsible for investigating the difficulties the child is experiencing in areas such as writing, spelling, phonological skills etc.

▶▶ **Continuum of difficulties**: Rather than fitting into a clear-cut category, a child's difficulties may be viewed along a continuum from mild to severe. This implies that the provision of learning support intervention may also vary along a continuum. Some children will need one-to-one attention for a period of time; others will benefit from small group teaching; others will work best with specially adapted materials in the main class. One size does not fit all.

REFERENCES

Cosgrove, J., Kellaghan, T., Forde, P., & Morgan, M. (2000). *The 1998 National Assessment of English Reading.* Dublin: Educational Research Centre.

Department of Education (1988). *Guidelines on Remedial Education.* Dublin: The Stationery Office.

Department of Education & Science (2000). *Learning Support Guidelines.* Dublin: Government Publications.

Hughes, A. (2000). *The School System and Specific Learning Disabilities/Dyslexia.* Dublin: Dyslexia Association of Ireland.

Ireland (1995). *Charting our Education Future: White Paper on Education.* Dublin: The Stationery Office.

Martin, M., & Morgan, M. (1994). *Reading Literacy in Irish Schools: A Comparative Analysis.* Irish Journal of Education, 28.

OECD/Statistics Canada. (2000). *Literacy in the information age. Final report of the International Adult Literacy Survey.* Paris: OECD/Ottawa: Statistics Canada.

Shiel, G., Morgan, M. & Larney, R. (1998). *Study of Remedial Education in Irish Primary Schools: Summary Report.* Dublin: Government Publications.

Special Education Review Committee. *Report.* (1993). Dublin: The Stationery Office.

Task Force on Dyslexia. (2002). Report. Dublin: Government Publications.

PART 1

SPECIFIC LEARNING DISABILITIES

Definitions, Characteristics and Implications

- SERC Report Review
- What is a Specific Learning Disability (SLD)?
- Characteristics of Children with Specific Learning Disabilities
- Approaches and Strategies — The Role of the LST

Specific Speech and Language Disorders

- Components of Language
- What can go wrong with language?
- Difficulties which may be evident in the classroom — comprehension, expressive, pragmatics
- The Relationship between Speech and Language Difficulties and the Acquisition of Written Language Skills
- Assessment of Language
- How to Help in the Classroom — Guidelines for Teachers
- Intervention by the Speech and Language Therapist

SERC REPORT REVIEW

The *Report of the Special Education Review Committee* (SERC/Ireland, 1993) described pupils with special needs in the following categories:

1. **Pupils with Learning Difficulties and Disorders**

    ▶▶   Pupils in need of remedial* teaching

    ▶▶   Pupils with Specific Learning Disabilities (SLDs)

    ▶▶   Pupils with Specific Speech and Language Disorders

2. **Pupils with Physical and Sensory Disabilities**

    ▶▶   Pupils with physical handicap**

    ▶▶   Pupils with hearing impairment

    ▶▶   Pupils with visual impairment

3. **Pupils with Mental Handicap*** and with Emotional and Behavioural Disorders**

    ▶▶   Pupils with mild mental handicap

    ▶▶   Pupils with moderate mental handicap

    ▶▶   Pupils with severe/profound mental handicap

    ▶▶   Pupils with emotional and/or behavioural disorders

    ▶▶   Pupils with childhood autism****

4. **Pupils with Other Special Needs**

    ▶▶   Pupils who are educationally and socially disadvantaged

    ▶▶   Children of the Travelling Community

    ▶▶   Pupils who are exceptionally able or talented

This manual addresses only those categories of special need referred to in Category 1.

These are:

▶▶   Pupils in need of remedial teaching (see section on Learning Support Guidelines, page 32)

▶▶   Pupils with Specific Learning Disabilities

▶▶   Pupils with Specific Speech and Language Disorders

* The term *learning support* has replaced *remedial* in recent years.

** The term *handicap* has now been replaced by *disability*.

*** The term now used widely is *General Learning Disabilities*.

**** The term *autistic spectrum disorder* is now the preferred term.

WHAT IS A SPECIFIC LEARNING DISABILITY (SLD)?

> *Specific learning disability is a term used to describe impairment in specific areas such as reading, writing and arithmetical notation, the primary cause of which is not attributable to assessed ability being below the average range, to defective sight or hearing, emotional factors, a physical condition or to any extrinsic adverse circumstances.*
>
> *(Report of the Special Education Review Committee, 1993, p. 86)*

Specific Learning Disability — SLD — is the term applied to those students whose learning difficulties are *not* due to lack of intelligence, sensory or motor disadvantage, or inadequate teaching.

The literature shows that approximately 2% of the school-going population in general has persistent and severe difficulties in attaining literacy skills. In Ireland in 1993, SERC reported an incidence of 0.3% of pupils who had been formally identified as having Specific Learning Disabilities. Identification of SLDs among pupils in Ireland appears to be remarkably low; there would seem to be an under-diagnosis of SLDs.

Dyslexia is sometimes described as a type of SLD. Other specific learning disabilities include:

▸ **Dysgraphia** — difficulties with writing

▸ **Dysorthographia** — difficulties with spelling

▸ **Dyscalculia** — difficulties with mathematics

However, such terms are not helpful in assisting teachers in their decisions about intervention and teaching strategies. Communication disorders such as specific Speech and Language Disorder comprise another subset of SLDs which will be addressed in this manual. The literature also refers to other Specific Learning Disabilities such as: Attention Deficit (Hyperactive) Disorder (ADHD), Developmental Coordination Disorder and Asperger Syndrome among others (Lerner, 2000; Westwood, 1997).

This manual will confine itself to those SLDs mentioned in Category 1, as referred to in the *SERC Report*.

CHARACTERISTICS OF CHILDREN WITH SPECIFIC LEARNING DISABILITIES

In the classroom, a teacher may notice a marked discrepancy between oral and written work. The child may seem brighter than his/her reading and written work suggests.

When a Specific Learning Disability is suspected, assessment by a psychologist using a standardised intelligence test is necessary. The main aim of such a test is to confirm that the child's ability is in the average range or higher. If the child's academic performance is much lower than expected, this may indeed suggest a Specific Learning Disability.

A child with SLD may exhibit one or many of the following characteristics.

ABILITY LEVEL OF CHILD

▸▸ *Average*: Is the child's intellectual ability in the average range for his/her age, based on his/her performance on a test of intelligence?

▸▸ *Above Average*: Does the child's performance on standardised intelligence tests place the child above the norm for his/her age?

SPEECH AND LANGUAGE DIFFICULTIES

▸▸ May have been a late or poor talker and may still have immature speech.

▸▸ May have word-finding difficulties — unable to name things and people (*verbal labelling*).

▸▸ May have problems understanding prepositions such as under/over, in front/behind.

▸▸ May have difficulty understanding mathematical terms such as difference, sum of, and total. About 60% of children with SLDs have difficulty with basic maths.

ORIENTATION DIFFICULTIES

Spatial Organisation

▸▸ May have a poor or excellent spatial ability; poor/excellent concept of space and size. (Careers in architecture, art and design, and engineering require good spatial ability.)

▸▸ May have difficulties understanding spatial concepts such as bigger/smaller, longer/shorter, further/nearer.

Temporal Concepts

▸▸ May be unable to understand concepts like before/after, now/then, today/tomorrow.

VISUAL PERCEPTUAL DIFFICULTIES

Visual Discrimination

▶▶ Unable to discriminate between visual stimuli — b/d, p/g, on/no

Visual Closure

▶▶ May be unable to fill in missing parts when only part of an object, letter or a word is seen.

Visual Figure-Ground

▶▶ May be unable to perceive a foreground figure against a background.

Visual Comprehension

▶▶ May be unable to recognise a familiar object.

AUDITORY PERCEPTUAL DIFFICULTIES

Auditory Discrimination

▶▶ Unable to discriminate between sounds — seem/seen, lemon/melon, mat/mad, wish/with.

Auditory Closure

▶▶ May be unable to recognise a word when a sound is omitted.

Auditory Comprehension

▶▶ May be unable to comprehend the spoken word.

Auditory Figure-Ground

▶▶ May be unable to attend to important auditory stimuli by pushing all other stimuli into the background.

These auditory skills are necessary for good phonological awareness.

MEMORY DIFFICULTIES

Visual Memory

▶▶ May be unable to remember and form a mental image (visualise) — poor spelling ability; poor ability to retain sight words.

Auditory Memory

▶▶ May be unable to remember and process auditory information or sequences. The child may therefore have problems: following complex verbal instructions; remembering days of the week, months of the year, seasons; alphabet; events of the day. Letter sequences in spelling may also present problems.

MOTOR DIFFICULTIES: COORDINATION

▶▶ May have poor fine and gross motor skills.

▶▶ May be uncoordinated; may be clumsy, awkward and accident-prone.

ATTENTION DIFFICULTIES: ATTENTION SPAN

▶▶ May have a poor concentration span or be inclined to dream.

▶▶ May be constantly distracted by comings and goings.

▶▶ May be unable to concentrate on any one task for very long.

ORGANISATIONAL DIFFICULTIES

▶▶ May have poor organisational skills; unable to manage self and belongings.

▶▶ May have a very poor approach to tasks, rushing through work carelessly.

▶▶ May use avoidance strategies to escape completing tasks.

ACTIVITY LEVEL

Hyperactive

▶▶ May be constantly in motion, jumping out of seat or skipping from task to task.

Hypoactive

▶▶ The opposite of hyperactivity; may appear lethargic and unresponsive.

EMOTIONAL/BEHAVIOURAL PROBLEMS

Social Competence

▶▶ Social skills may often be below average for age and ability.

Self-Esteem

▶▶ May have a very poor self concept and may feel worthless and inadequate.

Impulsive Behaviour

▶▶ May fail to stop and think about the consequences of behaviour.

Explosive

▶▶ May react aggressively to situations/throw tantrums.

(UCD Developmental Disabilities Course, author unknown)

When considering these characteristics, remember that no one will have *all* these symptoms. In addition, the *number of characteristics* observed in a particular child does not indicate whether the disability is mild or severe. Instead, consider whether the behaviours appear in a *cluster* and the way in which behaviour presents on a *continuum* from mild to severe.

APPROACHES AND STRATEGIES — THE ROLE OF THE LST

There is widespread agreement that early identification of Specific Learning Disabilities is of great importance. The *Learning Support Guidelines* (DES, 2000) recommend:

1. Preliminary screening of all pupils — ie administration and interpretation of screening measures by the class teacher.

2. Selection of pupils for diagnostic assessment following consultation with parents, teacher and LST.

3. Administering of diagnostic tests by LST.

The LST is responsible for coordinating a programme of supplementary teaching for a pupil who has been identified as having SLD. Information received from the educational psychologist's report, along with diagnostic assessment tests administered by the Learning Support Teacher, will outline the child's strengths and needs. All of this information creates an individual profile of the child. It will help in the planning process and in setting priorities for supplementary teaching, providing starting points for instruction.

As an underlying principle, this manual highlights the importance of the dynamic interaction between assessment and teaching, and between teaching and assessment. The LST will order the priorities for teaching based on diagnostic assessments of pupils, as well as on information gathered from other sources (class teacher, parents etc.). He/She will select a starting point for teaching based on these needs.

Reid (1998, pp. 34, 35) recommends that a broad range of assessment strategies should be used to identify children with SLDs. According to Reid, assessment should consider these three aspects:

▸▸ difficulties

▸▸ discrepancies

▸▸ differences

For example, the child's central *difficulty* may:

▸▸ be related to the decoding or encoding of print

▸▸ involve phonological processing difficulties

▸▸ include memory problems or language difficulties

A *discrepancy* may be apparent between oral and written language, or between reading and listening comprehension.

Individual *differences* among pupils must be recognised in the assessment, along with an appreciation of individual learning styles, and individual strengths and needs.

The LST's diagnostic testing may include areas such as assessing the child's phonological awareness, analysing his/her miscues in written language, and observing his/her individual learning style.

For further information on Diagnostic Testing, see Part 2, page 42.

Refer also to The Role of the Learning Support Teacher, pp. 32-34.

SPECIFIC SPEECH AND LANGUAGE DISORDERS

In compiling this section, the author acknowledges: Aoife Byrne, Principal Speech & Language Therapist, East Coast Area Health Board; Mary Scullion, Senior Speech & Language Therapist, Lucena Clinic; and Abigail Whyte, Senior Clinical Psychologist, Lucena Clinic.

COMPONENTS OF LANGUAGE

Language can be broken down into a number of basic component parts.

COMPREHENSION — Ability to understand what is being said.

Imagine being in Germany with no idea of the language. How would you cope? This provides some idea of the frustration which a child might feel when s/he has a specific language comprehension difficulty.

EXPRESSION — Ability to convey messages through spoken language.

Includes using appropriate words, combinations of words and grammatical structures.

PRONUNCIATION — Ability to articulate sounds and words.

USE — Ability to use and respond to language appropriately, eg keeping on track in a conversation and not going off on tangents; recognising other people's intentions; using background information.

Possible Difficulties

Example 1

The child says: "She went to the cinema" without previously specifying who "she" is.

Example 2

Teacher: "How old are you, Johnny?"

Johnny: "I'm seven and I got a tennis racket yesterday and then last year I got a bike and then soon I'm going to get a dog and all my friends came and daddy was sick…" etc. etc. etc.

WHAT CAN GO WRONG WITH LANGUAGE?

Not every child who exhibits two or three of the following difficulties will have a language problem which requires attention. However, when a child exhibits a significant number of these, and where academic progress is uneven, the child should be considered for referral.

It is important to note that children who have depressed language and academic skills, particularly those who appear to be generally immature, are more likely to have a general learning disability. Their language skills are likely to be in line with their overall intellectual ability.

It is those children who have an uneven scatter of language and academic abilities who are appropriate candidates for SLD screening (or assessment).

Children with specific language disorders can experience the following difficulties.

▶▶ *Delayed language skills* — One or more components of language are delayed for the child's age, although developmental stages are otherwise normal.

▶▶ *Disordered language development* — This is characterised by an uneven scatter of language abilities which are significantly disproportionate to skills in other areas; not caused by hearing difficulties, general learning disability, physical disability (eg cerebral palsy, cleft palate) or primary emotional difficulties.

▶▶ *Difficulty in one or all of the language components* — Comprehension, Expression, Pronunciation or Use of Language.

DIFFICULTIES WHICH MAY BE EVIDENT IN THE CLASSROOM

1. COMPREHENSION DIFFICULTIES

Typical comprehension difficulties such as the following may be evident in the classroom.

▶▶ **DIFFICULTY FOLLOWING A SERIES OF INSTRUCTIONS**

Examples

At school — Child may have difficulty following instructions from teacher during PE or on the playing field.

At home — Child is sent upstairs to look for something, then forgets what s/he was sent to find.

▶▶ **DIFFICULTIES WITH LEFT/RIGHT ORIENTATION**

Examples

"Write the day on the top left-hand side of your page and your name on the bottom right."

"The red team — move to the left side of the court. The blues — move forward."

▶▶ **LIMITED UNDERSTANDING OF VOCABULARY**

Example

"…the Secretary's office opposite the library in the Junior School…"

▶▶ **TAKING COMMON PHRASES OR HUMOUR LITERALLY**

Examples

"She has green fingers."

"My mother has eyes in the back of her head."

"It's right under your nose!"

"It's raining cats and dogs."

▶▶ **DIFFICULTIES WITH CONCEPT WORDS SUCH AS BEFORE, AFTER, FIRST, LAST**

Example

"**If** you haven't finished your picture **before** the bell rings, you can finish it **after** the break."

▶▶ **ZONING IN ON ONE OR TWO FAMILIAR WORDS IN A SENTENCE WITHOUT GRASPING THE OVERALL MEANING**

Example

Teacher: "If any of you are going to be absent for a few extra days because of holidays, let me know in advance so I can arrange to give your parents some work for you."

Child: "Where are we going?"

▶▶ **MEMORY DIFFICULTIES**

Examples

Child may not be able to repeat messages. When s/he takes a telephone call, s/he may forget the name of speaker. When given the message "Dad will be home late because he has missed the train. He'll be on the next one", the child may only remember the "Dad will be late" part.

▶▶ **COMPREHENSION AND EXPRESSIVE DIFFICULTIES CAUSING EMOTIONAL OR BEHAVIOURAL ISSUES**

Temper tantrums or physical aggression in the playground may be caused by misunderstandings among peers. Because these children do not have the language with which to talk about their feelings, they may act out in defiance or become victims of bullying.

Example

The child may say "He pushed me" instead of explaining that "…he bumped into me because he was running and didn't see me".

A child with language delay may experience stress and frustration in communicating with others. As a result, s/he may become shy or withdrawn.

▶▶ **DIFFICULTIES UNDERSTANDING RULES: SCHOOL RULES, RULES FOR GAMES**

Example

"You can run after me until you catch me, but if John goes under my legs, I'm free."

▶▶ **DIFFICULTY IN RELAYING MESSAGES OUTSIDE CLASSROOM**

Example

Teacher: "Go to Room 2 and ask the teacher to send in Mark."

Child goes to Room 2 and brings back two markers.

▶▶ **DIFFICULTY WITH MORE COMPLEX QUESTION FORMS SUCH AS WHEN? HOW? WHY? WHO?**

Example

Adult: "When did you go swimming?"

Child: "With my daddy."

▶▶ **SIMPLY REPEATING PART OF A SENTENCE/QUESTION**

When this occurs, chances are the child did not understand the question.

Example

Adult: "Where is your homework from last night?"

Child: "Homework last night?"

2. EXPRESSIVE DIFFICULTIES

Typical difficulties such as the following may be apparent in the classroom.

▶▶ **WORD-FINDING DIFFICULTIES**

Examples

" Can I have that thing? The thing we bring on holidays with a light in it and you carry it in a little bag... you know, the thing you say 'Cheese' at."

"...the thing you look in to see yourself" instead of "mirror".

▶▶ **TELEGRAMMATIC SPEECH**

Example

"I go bed early tired."

▶▶ **POOR STORY-TELLING ABILITY WITH NO OBVIOUS SEQUENCE**

Example

Adult: "Tell me about the trip to the zoo yesterday."

Child: "We went home after, my bag broke, Ann was on the bus…"

▶▶ **EXHIBITS GRAMMATICAL DIFFICULTIES**

Example

"The cat **sitted** on the mat." "She **teached** me."

▶▶ **POOR ABILITY TO GIVE EXAMPLES FROM A CATEGORY OR IDENTIFY THE CATEGORY**

Can you name a fruit? A piece of furniture? A farm animal?

What's an apple? What's a chair?

▶▶ **PROBLEMS WITH CAUSE AND EFFECT**

Example 1

Adult: "What would you do if you saw a robber?"

Child: "He's robbing my house."

Example 2

Adult: "What should you do if you lose a ball that belongs to one of your friends?"

Child: "Give it back to him."

▶▶ **TEND NOT TO VOLUNTEER INFORMATION IN CLASS**

Unable to sustain the topic under discussion. Unable to extend the topic of conversation.

▶▶ **TAKE A LONG TIME TO GET THEIR MESSAGE ACROSS**

Inadequate language structures used by the child — difficulties with verb tenses, plurals etc. Child relies on short, incomplete utterances.

3. DIFFICULTY WITH LANGUAGE USE (PRAGMATICS)

Difficulties such as these may be apparent in the classroom.

▶▶ **IRRELEVANT OR INAPPROPRIATE UTTERANCES**

What the child says is not relevant or appropriate to the situation, context or people present.

Example

Out of the blue, the child says: "She went to the pictures."

▶▶ **MAY HAVE DIFFICULTY WITH TURN-TAKING OR LISTENER-SPEAKER RELATIONSHIP**

Example

Constantly interrupts, doesn't read signals.

▶▶ **DIFFICULTY WITH EYE CONTACT**

▶▶ **DIFFICULTY STAYING ON TOPIC. MAY GO OFF ON TANGENTS**

Example

Teacher: "What did you see at the zoo?"

Child: "We went on Wednesday and it was wet and we have an umbrella at home and my granny gave me a ball to play with."

▶▶ **USES LANGUAGE FOR ONLY A LIMITED NUMBER OF INTENTIONS**

Example

Can't use language to tell jokes, predict outcomes, or express needs and feelings.

Limited in using language to explain, to imagine, to recognise the central meaning.

THE RELATIONSHIP BETWEEN SPEECH AND LANGUAGE DIFFICULTIES AND THE ACQUISITION OF WRITTEN LANGUAGE SKILLS

Language is generally seen as a code by which our thoughts and ideas are expressed through symbols, ie words. These words can be in the form of *spoken words* (*primary language system*) or *written words* (*secondary language system*). Any difficulty in acquiring the primary language system often has significant implications in acquiring a secondary language system. Research shows that where a child's language difficulties extend beyond the age of 5.5 years, the child is at risk of going on to exhibit difficulties with the acquisition of reading/writing skills (Lees & Urwin 1991). The main areas of difficulty are:

▸▸ Poorly developed phonological awareness skills

▸▸ Relating written word to their "store" of words. Poorly developed phonological awareness skills make it difficult to manage tasks such as the following which are necessary for the acquisition of spoken words as well as written language:

    ▸▸ breaking down words into syllables

    ▸▸ blending syllables into words

    ▸▸ breaking syllables into phonemes/blending phonemes into syllables

▸▸ Recognising "real" words as opposed to "nonsense" words

▸▸ Appreciation of rhyme

WORD-FINDING DIFFICULTIES (ANOMIA)

This does not refer to a difficulty with vocabulary as such, but to the retrieval of stored words (the "tip of my tongue" feeling). Low frequency words and polysyllabic words cause most difficulty.

Children with dyslexia often find it difficult to retrieve "stored information" or written words from their long-term memory and so may make errors on what appear to be basic tasks.

SEQUENCING DIFFICULTIES

Children with language difficulties and children with dyslexia often exhibit difficulties with sequencing tasks: learning nursery rhymes, number sequences, days of the week, months etc. This clearly has implications for their ability to remember sequences of letters.

SEVERE ARTICULATION DIFFICULTIES (DYSPRAXIA)

A severe difficulty in the production of words affects the child's ability to rehearse words which, in turn, leads to inaccurate storage of words, and therefore to inaccurate attempts to spell words. Spelling attempts may differ — the child may not always make the same error.

ASSESSMENT OF LANGUAGE

A child may have difficulties with *articulation or pronunciation* of language, with *receptive* language or with *expressive* language.

ARTICULATION AND PRONUNCIATION

Articulation problems tend to be more easily recognisable and are identified earlier by parents and pre-school teachers.

▶▶ Does the child say very few words by the age of two years?

▶▶ Are the phrases and speech of a three-year-old child unintelligible to his/her primary carer?

▶▶ Is the child's speech unintelligible by the age of four?

▶▶ Does the child mispronounce words or substitute sounds by the age of seven?

If the answer to all these questions is "Yes", the child should be referred to a speech therapist for assessment.

RECEPTIVE LANGUAGE

Receptive language involves understanding spoken language. Children with language comprehension difficulties often do not come to the attention of parents and teachers until reading and spelling difficulties are apparent. Reading and spelling skills are dependent on the child's ability to use spoken language.

A child with receptive language difficulties will have problems understanding verbal directions and may misinterpret instructions.

▶▶ Hearing difficulties should be ruled out first as a causative factor.

▶▶ The child should have an in-depth language assessment which focuses on all areas of language functioning.

▶▶ Intellectual assessment which examines the discrepancies between verbal and performance IQ scores is often indicated. Performance IQ should be within the average range of ability, thus providing ideas of potential intellectual functioning.

▶▶ Other areas to explore include: emotional and social development; motor control; attention span; family history of learning difficulties.

When a child is being considered for referral, it is worth remembering that children with seemingly pure language difficulties would be seen in Community Care clinics, whereas children with additional behavioural/emotional difficulties would be seen in Child Guidance clinics.

EXPRESSIVE LANGUAGE

Some children with *expressive language difficulties*:

▶▶   will have poor vocabulary

▶▶   will experience difficulty in naming familiar people, places and objects

▶▶   may use incorrect grammar and poor syntax.

Receptive and expressive language difficulties present problems when the child enters school where 75% of the day is spent in listening and speaking.

HOW TO HELP IN THE CLASSROOM

GUIDELINES FOR TEACHERS

The following suggestions are specifically focussed on the areas of language difficulty which may present in the classroom.

Comprehension: Words such as "before", "after", "if", "except" may be difficult for the child to comprehend. Demonstrate the meaning of these words in a simple fashion.

Examples

"We eat our breakfast *before* we come to school."

"We all go swimming *except* Mammy."

Following Directions: Before a child can comprehend directions such as, "If you have not finished question 4 by the time the bell rings, you can finish it after the break", s/he must first comprehend the various concept words used.

Examples

▸▸ Play "Simple Simon says… Take two steps forward, then sit down." This helps with direction and orientation.

▸▸ Teach a child to *give* instructions — eg choose a familiar possession such as a video recorder and ask: "How do you use it?" Bike — "How do you mend a puncture?"

▸▸ Favourite food — "How do you make scrambled eggs? Beans on toast?"

Memory Games: These games help to develop auditory sequential memory.

Examples

"I went to the supermarket and I bought…"

"Tom had a birthday and he got a book, felt tip pens…"

Passive Sentences: Check that the child understands sentences such as:

"John was beaten by Peter." / "Who was beaten?"

"The rat was eaten by the cat" / "What was eaten?"

Limited Vocabulary: Use every opportunity to expand the child's vocabulary.

▶▶ Teach child how to describe an object. A few key questions can be asked to describe a sock, a chair, a bicycle: 'What is it made from? What shape is it? What size is it? How do we use it?'

▶▶ Teach child to describe a person. Pretend s/he has to make a photo-fit picture of a bank robber. Useful words to describe a person include: figure, face/head, nose, forehead, hair, eyes, skin, mouth/lips/teeth, character, clothes, voice, age…

▶▶ Name as many items as possible from different categories — fruit, things we buy in bottles etc.

Word-Finding: Describe an object without naming it. The child must guess what the object is. This includes "I spy" / "What am I?" games.

Examples

"I have numbers on my face. I have two hands. I sometimes chime. What am I?" (a clock)

"I am hot. I sometimes spray or give off steam. I move over clothes. What am I?" (an iron)

Work on categories and classification.

Examples

Labrador — Collie — Terrier / Tulips — Daffodils — Roses

Ask child to name four different drinks, sports or vegetables.

▶▶ Play "Silly Sentences". The child has to repeat the sentence, say what is wrong and give a suitable word in its place.

    Examples

    "The telephone is singing"

    "The shop sailed out to sea."

▶▶ Play "Rhyming Sentences". Sentences with an integral rhyme help the awareness of similar sounding words. Ask the child to fill in the missing rhyme.

    The **nurse** had a _____ (purse)

    The **fish** is on the _____ (dish)

    We will go on a **train** to _____ (Spain)

▶▶ Odd-one-out can be played with pictures or objects — pear/book/biscuit/bread.

▶▶ Similarities/differences: "Tell me all the differences between summer and winter." "How are cars and trains alike?"

Time Sequences: Practise sequences such as days of the week, months, seasons etc.

Poor Sequencing: Retell simple incidents such as "A Visit to Granny". Ensure that the sequence of actions is correct. Cut out a picture and ask the child to tell you about it. Help him/her to tell you what happened *before* and *after* the picture was taken or drawn.

Grammatical Difficulties: If a particular point of grammar is constantly incorrect, put the child in the situation of hearing the correct structure a few times in sequence. Then encourage him/her to make up a few sentences using the particular structure.

INTERVENTION BY THE SPEECH AND LANGUAGE THERAPIST

Once a child's difficulties have been diagnosed, therapy is initiated. This may involve purely speech and language therapy, or it could be a combination of language therapy, individual psychotherapy or parent management work.

Speech and language therapists rely on parental involvement to facilitate the carry-over from formal therapy sessions and to influence progress. This therapy can be given in individual or group settings, depending on the child's needs or the resources available.

Before therapy starts, it is difficult to predict how far a child will progress. While some children will close the gap between intellectual ability and language levels, others will reach a plateau at some stage. When this occurs, children will need further coping strategies.

A multi-disciplinary approach is the most effective way for progress to be sustained over time: that is, when responsibility and expertise are shared among language therapist, teacher and parents to promote the language development of the child.

A good oral language programme in school, as well as teachers who are sensitive to the needs of the child with language difficulties, will also help. *The English Language: Teacher Guidelines of The Primary School Curriculum* (DES, 1999) recognises the development of oral language skills as central to effective communication.

The child learns primarily through language, using language to clarify images and to organise concepts and ideas. Through daily oral language activities in class, the teacher fosters competence and confidence in using language as a speaker and as a listener.

Children with severe speech and language difficulties, however, will need speech and language therapy. Some children will need regular sessions of intensive language therapy to remediate particular difficulties. However, the reality is that there is a shortage of qualified Speech and Language Therapists. In addition, some families drop out of therapy.

An individualised programme of therapy can be very effective for children who need regular one-to-one sessions with the therapist. Language deficiencies *can* be remedied. Follow-up with parents and liaison with the child's teacher are recommended.

REFERENCES

Department of Education & Science (1999). *Primary School Curriculum: English, Teacher Guidelines.* Dublin: The Stationery Office.

Department of Education & Science (2000). *Learning Support Guidelines*. Dublin: The Stationery Office.

Howlin & Rutter, M. (1981). *Language Development and Disorders*. In R. Barkley, *The consequences of language delay for other aspects of development.* London: McKeith Press.

Lees, J. & Urwin, S. (1991). *Children with Language Disorders.* London: Whurr.

Lerner, J. (1983). *Learning Disabilities.* Boston: Houghton Mifflin Company.

Reid, G. (1998). *Dyslexia: A Practitioner's Handbook.* England: John Wiley & Sons.

Special Education Review Committee (1993). *Report.* Dublin: The Stationery Office.

University College Dublin. *Handout from Developmental Disabilities Course* (author unknown)

Westwood, P. (1993). *Commonsense Methods for Children with Special Needs.* London: Routledge.

PART 2

LEARNING SUPPORT

- Whole School Policy for Learning Support
- The Role of the Learning Support Teacher
- Learning Support Intervention
- Screening in Context — by Bríd Clancy/NEPS
- Diagnostic Assessment
- The Individual Education Plan
- The National Educational Psychological Service (NEPS) — by Bríd Clancy/NEPS

The author wishes to acknowledge Bríd Clancy/NEPS for contributing "Screening in Context" and "The National Educational Psychological Service" to this section.

WHOLE SCHOOL POLICY FOR LEARNING SUPPORT

Every school is now required to have a school policy on learning support. The Education Act (1998), Section 9, states that the functions of a school must "*ensure that the educational needs of students, including those with disability or special needs, are identified and provided* for" (p. 13).

This policy should be drawn up in consultation with the "partners" in education: the board of management, principal teacher, class teachers, learning support teacher(s) (LSTs) and parents. It should state the beliefs and principles of learning support according to the *Learning Support Guidelines* (DES, 2000), and should include the aims or "mission statement" of the school according to its own individual ethos and beliefs.

THE ROLE OF THE LEARNING SUPPORT TEACHER

The role of the Learning Support Teacher (LST) is outlined in detail in the *Learning Support Guidelines* (DES, 2000).

The key tasks in defining this role are *collaboration* and *consultation* with all the partners involved, ie the class teachers, principal, parents, students and outside agencies.

In the context of the whole school policy on learning support, the LST will:

▸▸ *Contribute* to school policy development.

▸▸ *Assist* in whole school early intervention/prevention.

▸▸ *Advise* staff on selection, use and interpretation of standardised tests.

▸▸ *Consult* with class teachers on selection of pupils for diagnostic assessment.

As noted in the Introduction (page 1), this approach reiterates the recommendation in the *Guidelines on Remedial Education* (Department of Education, 1988) which urged a team approach, with the "remedial" teacher in a consultative role.

The *Learning Support Guidelines* (DES, 2000) include further information on collaboration between the LST and other partners involved, ie principal, class teachers and parents. While these collaborative and consultative activities are essential to the whole school policy on Learning Support, the main focus of the LST's work will be on providing *supplementary teaching* to pupils. This supplementary teaching may be provided either by withdrawing the child for learning support or by different shared teaching approaches. The LST will refer closely to the elements of Learning Support as outlined in these guidelines.

LEARNING SUPPORT INTERVENTION

The principal aim of learning support is to optimise the teaching and learning process in order to enable pupils with learning difficulties to achieve adequate levels of proficiency in literacy and numeracy before leaving primary school.

(*Learning Support Guidelines*, 2000, p. 15)

The recommended sequence for screening, selection, diagnostic assessment, programme planning, programme implementation and programme review is set out in a flowchart on page 60 in the *Learning Support Guidelines* (2000).

Screening is the first step in identifying pupils who are underachieving in the areas of literacy and mathematics. Screening the whole school will identify those pupils in need of supplementary teaching. According to the *Learning Support Guidelines*, those pupils achieving at or below the 10th percentile in literacy and mathematics may be selected for further diagnostic assessment. This diagnostic assessment would be carried out by the LST in consultation with the class teacher.

ELEMENTS OF LEARNING SUPPORT INTERVENTION

1. Preliminary Screening
Administration and interpretation of screening measure(s) by the class teacher

▼

2. Selection for Diagnostic Assessment
Application of cut-off score
Consultation between the class teacher and parents
Consultation between the class teacher and LST

▼

3. Diagnostic Assessment
Administration of diagnostic tests by the LST
Interpretation of the outcomes of the assessment in consultation with the class teacher

▼

4. Decision to Provide Supplementary Teaching
Meeting between LST and parents
Development of the Individual Profile and Learning Programme (IPLP) by the LST, in consultation with the child's class teacher

▼

5A. Modified Teaching Approach by Class Teacher
Appropriate modification of teaching approaches by the pupil's class teacher in the mainstream class

5B. Supplementary Teaching by the Learning Support Teacher
Provision of supplementary teaching in the classroom or in the learning-support room for an instructional term (13 to 20 weeks)
Planning and recording on the Weekly Planning and Progress Record (WPPR)

▼

6. Review of Progress at End of the Instructional Term
Assessment of child's progress
Evaluation of learning programme
Consultation between the LST, class teacher and parents to determine the level of support now required by the child

▼

7A. Discontinuation of Supplementary Teaching
Continuation of appropriate support in mainstream class and at home

7B. Continuation of Supplementary Teaching for a Further Instructional Term
Return to Step 4 above and repeat Steps 4 to 7

Screening In Context

Bríd Clancy/NEPS

While *Part One* of each school's plan is concerned with the curriculum, *Part Two* must set out its policies regarding administrative aspects of school life. *Developing a School Plan — Guidelines for Primary Schools* (DES, 1999*)* sets out the range of policies which each school should consider, including "the provision for pupils with special needs" (p. 23) and "the recording and dissemination of information related to pupil progress" (p. 24).

For most schools, screening is the first stage in identifying children with special needs. This will be followed by diagnostic assessment by the LST and, where necessary, further assessment by external agents such as the educational psychologist, speech therapist, occupational therapist or clinical psychologist.

In devising the school's screening policy, consider these six simple questions.

> **WHY** are we testing?
>
> **WHAT** should we test?
>
> **WHICH** tests should we use?
>
> **WHO** is responsible for what?
>
> **WHEN** should we test?
>
> **WHAT** do we do NOW?

WHY are we testing?

The school's reasons for screening may include the following:

▸▸ Identify children who are underachieving and who may need learning support in literacy and maths.

▸▸ Identify children who may have *specific* or *general* learning difficulties.

▸▸ Identify children who may be entitled to resource-hour allocation under *DES Circulars 8/99* and *8/02*.

▶▶ Identify children who are achieving very highly but who may need greater differentiation of the curriculum.

▶▶ Obtain hard data which will assist in communicating progress to parents.

▶▶ Obtain statistical information for measuring school success in relation to local, regional and national level in order to inform policy and practice.

WHAT SHOULD WE TEST?

LITERACY

▶▶ Reading attainment should be tested. In doing so, schools must be clear about which aspect of reading is being assessed: pre-reading skills, single word decoding, reading in context, reading comprehension. Decisions should be made at whole school level regarding which aspect(s) to test at each grade level and which tests are most appropriate for this purpose.

▶▶ Spelling

▶▶ Written expression

MATHS

▶▶ Computation

▶▶ Problem-solving

▶▶ Tables

GENERAL ABILITY

▶▶ Verbal Reasoning *and/or*

▶▶ Non-verbal Reasoning

AFFECTIVE, SOCIAL AND EMOTIONAL DEVELOPMENT

▶▶ The DES document *Developing a School Plan — Guidelines for Primary Schools* (DES, 1999, p. 36) advocates "qualitative assessment in the affective, social and emotional development of the child and in those areas of the curriculum that do not lend themselves to quantitative marking schemes".

▸▸ The school may generate checklists of core skills against which children can be screened through teacher observation. A useful pool of such targets is available at http://www.users.globalnet.co.uk. Checklists are particularly useful for Infant classes and can be extended to include language development, self-esteem, metacognitive strategies and learning style.

▸▸ The school psychologist might be consulted when generating such checklists.

WHICH TESTS SHOULD WE USE?

Any test selected should:

▸▸ Strike a balance between efficiency, practicality (quick, used with groups, easy to administer and score) and high accuracy.

▸▸ Have high validity: it should measure what you intend it to measure. For example, if you wish to test word decoding, avoid assessment tools which really test comprehension.

▸▸ Suitable for the target age range/stage.

▸▸ Be well-established, respected, current and reliable.

ADDITIONALLY, FOR CLASSES I TO VI

▸▸ Offer normative data: standard scores and percentile ranks which allow comparison with the general population.

▸▸ Standardised on an Irish sample.

...AND, FOR INFANTS

▸▸ Criterion-referenced: tests the degree to which a child has achieved certain skills rather than offering standard scores or percentile ranks.

▸▸ Developed for use with an Irish population.

WHO IS RESPONSIBLE FOR WHAT?

The *Learning Support Guidelines* describe the following responsibilities in the area of screening.

THE CLASS TEACHER

Described as "the first line of responsibility", the *Learning Support Guidelines* state that the class teacher will take responsibility for the following:

▶▶ Administering screening tests to his or her class.

▶▶ Scoring test scripts and interpreting results.

▶▶ Consulting with the Learning Support Teacher on the selection of children for diagnostic assessment (based on pre-determined criteria, cut-off points etc.).

▶▶ Meeting with parents to provide feedback on screening.

▶▶ Explaining school policy and procedures to parents.

▶▶ Obtaining consent for diagnostic assessment.

THE LEARNING SUPPORT TEACHER

▶▶ Acts as co-ordinator, in lieu of the principal. (Alternatively, this role may be assigned to another member of staff.)

▶▶ Has a core role in policy development.

▶▶ Must liaise closely with principal.

▶▶ Advises staff on the selection of screening instruments.

▶▶ Advises staff on the scoring and interpretation of these instruments.

▶▶ Consults with class teacher on the selection of children for diagnostic assessment.

THE PRINCIPAL TEACHER

▶▶ Co-ordinates learning support and special needs services, including initial screening (although part of this role may be delegated to another member of staff).

▶▶ Takes overall responsibility for development and implementation of relevant policies.

▶▶ Oversees the school's screening and assessment programme.

▶▶ Monitors the selection of pupils for diagnostic assessment.

▶▶ Keeps staff informed about external assessment agencies and referral procedures.

THE BOARD OF MANAGEMENT

▶▶ Oversees the development, implementation and review of relevant policies.

▶▶ Provides secure facilities for the storage of records.

WHEN SHOULD WE TEST?

When tests specify the time of year at which they must be administered, such instructions should be adhered to carefully. As most tests do not make such specifications, the individual school must decide when to administer screening tests. The advantages and disadvantages of each should be discussed and the reasons for this choice stated in the overall school policy.

SCREENING EARLY IN THE SCHOOL YEAR (SEPTEMBER/OCTOBER)

▶▶ Offers a baseline of attainment prior to teaching (tends to be *formative* rather than *summative*).

▶▶ Meets the obligation for a school plan to "emphasise the need for teachers to assess pupils with a definite purpose in mind", and for decisions taken as a result "to lead to action" (DES, 1999, p. 37).

▶▶ Allows correction of scripts by the class teacher, thus facilitating qualitative verification of results.

▶▶ Measures medium-term retention of concepts and skills over the summer break, thus offering a more valid assessment of "real" learning.

▶▶ May be less likely to elicit false negatives (ie failing to identify a child who actually has a difficulty).

▶▶ May overestimate the prevalence of learning difficulties in the school.

▶▶ May prevent assessment results being used inadvertently to measure teacher effectiveness.

SCREENING AT THE END OF THE SCHOOL YEAR

▶▶ Planning for the next year may be done well in advance, allowing supplementary teaching to commence from early September.

▶▶ Recognises that children have settled into school routine and that test performance is less likely to be contaminated by low motivation or test anxiety.

▶▶ May facilitate testing of skills and concepts actually learned rather than those forgotten.

▶▶ May be less likely to elicit false positives (ie less likely to identify a child as having a difficulty who does not actually have such a difficulty).

▶▶ May underestimate the prevalence of learning difficulties in the school.

WHAT DO WE DO NOW?

ESTABLISH THE VALIDITY OF RESULTS

Once all children have been assessed, it is vital that the results are validated by the relevant class teachers. In so doing, human errors and other pitfalls should be considered and discounted. If a group of children appears to have underachieved, consider the following pitfalls:

▸▸ Was the wrong level of a particular test used?

▸▸ Was there inadequate preparation of the room, materials and children? Was rapport established? Did the children know what was required of them? Was the test interrupted by external factors? noise, visitors etc.?

▸▸ Were the standard administration instructions adhered to? (Did the administrator offer additional help?)

▸▸ Was the test administered at an inappropriate time (near a holiday, too close to lunch-time, immediately following a school trip or event)?

▸▸ Was a test used which did not correspond to the language of instruction in the school?

If an individual child achieved an unexpectedly low score, consider the following:

▸▸ Was the child absent for part of the test?

▸▸ Did the child fail to complete the script?

▸▸ Were there extenuating circumstances specific to the particular child on the day of the test (eg illness, an upset, a family difficulty)?

▸▸ Does the child have a sensory difficulty (hearing or vision)?

▸▸ Does the child have an emotional and/or behavioural difficulty which may have interfered with test performance (eg Attention Deficit Disorder, test anxiety, *very* low self-esteem, depression)?

▸▸ Does the child function poorly in group situations? (This may be particularly relevant for children with Asperger's Syndrome.)

▸▸ Should we reconsider the test validity for the individual child? (eg The Non-Reading Intelligence Test is likely to be particularly challenging for children with dyslexia and may be totally inappropriate for a child for whom English is an additional language. The standardisation sample may not represent children from minority groups such as the Travelling Community. Such children may require extra support although not necessarily for the reasons suggested by low test scores.)

▸▸ Are scores consistent? Compare the child's performance across maths, reading and general ability (eg NRIT) tests.

RECORD AND STORE RESULTS APPROPRIATELY

School policy must describe how results will be recorded. It must also state where this information will be stored so that it can be accessed easily by the principal, inspector and other relevant personnel. It is useful to create a database (manual or electronic) of all results to ease comparison between children and between different test results for an individual child. It is more useful to record standard scores and percentile ranks than test ages alone.

COMMUNICATE THE RESULTS TO PARENTS

How, when and by whom results are to be communicated to parents must be outlined — not only in relation to those children who are being recommended for further diagnostic assessment by the LST, but in relation to all children.

FOLLOW-UP: A CONTINUUM OF PROVISION

Although a child may not be eligible for learning support, testing may have indicated some relative underachievement which requires support within the mainstream classroom. Such children should not be overlooked; nor should screening become merely a method of selecting children for additional teaching outside the mainstream classroom.

Similarly, children who are achieving very highly may need careful consideration when the class teacher is planning his/her maths or literacy programmes. The NRIT provides a very useful table which compares attainment scores and ability scores, allowing those children who are significantly underachieving in literacy and maths to be identified.

For those children who are being recommended for further assessment, the *Learning Support Guidelines* make the following points:

▶▶ Any decisions must be made in collaboration with parents.

▶▶ Children at or below the 10th percentile rank must be offered learning support.

▶▶ Follow-up diagnostic assessment is required. In order to identify targets for the child's Individual Profile and Learning Programme (sometimes called an Individualised Education Plan or IEP), such assessment should be criterion-referenced rather than normative only.

Following further assessment by a psychologist or other external professionals, *Circular 8/02* should be consulted to identify children who may be entitled to resource teaching hours.

DIAGNOSTIC ASSESSMENT

> ➠ Introduction
>
> ➠ Important Underlying Principles of Identification and Assessment
>
> ➠ Diagnostic Assessment at Emergent Literacy Stage
>
> ➠ Diagnostic Assessment Beyond Early Literacy

INTRODUCTION

Once low achievement or a learning problem has been identified following screening procedures (see "Screening in Context", p. 35), the LST will consult the class teacher regarding which children require further testing. Parents will also be consulted. The LST will carry out individual tests to explore the child's learning strengths and needs. This process is called *diagnostic assessment*.

The purpose of this more comprehensive, individualised assessment is to obtain a picture of the child's learning profile, his/her skills, attainments, learning style and learning needs.

IMPORTANT UNDERLYING PRINCIPLES OF IDENTIFICATION AND ASSESSMENT

➠ *Individualisation of Assessment:* There is strong belief that children's needs should be assessed on an individual basis and provision made for them with a focus on individual learning needs. In the past, some children had to wait until they failed in the school system before coming to the notice of outside agencies. A whole school policy on learning support which involves assessment, intervention and regular review should redress this practice. The *Report of the Task Force on Dyslexia* (2002) views dyslexia as a "continuum" from mild to severe and favours an "individualised" model of assessment and provision of support according to the individual's needs.

➠ *Learning Support Guidelines* (DES, 2000): These guidelines now require Learning Support Teachers to review progress at the end of an instructional term. The primary purpose of this review is to determine whether or not learning targets have been achieved and to collaborate with the class teacher and principal regarding further supplementary teaching or referral for psychological assessment where considered necessary.

▶▶ *Individual Difference, Individual Preference, Learning Style*: Each child is unique. Assessment should take into account the individual strengths of the child and his/her preferred learning style.

▶▶ *Continuum of Difficulty*: Since children's needs range from the mild to the severe, the response to this need should therefore vary according to need. In other words, "one size" does not fit all. There is a danger in categories and labels.

▶▶ *Early Intervention*: The earlier the intervention, the better the outcome for the child and the more cost-effective it is to schools.

▶▶ *Differentiation of Teaching — Notice and Adjust*: Some children on the "mild" end of the continuum of difficulty will not require "specialised" outside help but will make progress *from skilled teacher interaction* and *adjustment of classroom teaching*.

▶▶ *Age of child*: The age of the child must be taken into account, along with his/her stage of development and realistic expectations at each stage.

▶▶ *Difficulties, Discrepancies, Differences:* A broadly based assessment is necessary to get a profile of the child. Diagnostic testing will provide the information which is necessary for planning learning support.

DIAGNOSTIC ASSESSMENT AT EMERGENT LITERACY STAGE

SENIOR INFANTS TO 1ST CLASS

The range of diagnostic tests used will depend on the child's age and level of development. At the early reading or *emergent literacy stage*, the following areas may be assessed.

▶▶ Print awareness — Is the child aware of print in the environment? (eg signs, labels etc.)

▶▶ Understanding the conventions of print — Written language progresses from left to right; top to bottom; distinguishing between letters, words and sentences.

▶▶ Phonemic awareness — Ability to recognise that rhyming words are composed of individual sounds; identify rhyming words; blending sounds to form words.

▶▶ Knowledge of letter sounds.

▶▶ Letter identification — letter/symbol/sound correspondence.

▶▶ Word recognition — Reading single words in isolation.

▶▶ Visual discrimination; auditory discrimination.

▶▶ Word identification skills; word attack skills.

▶▶ Comprehension of words and sentences.

▶▶ Spelling (approximate).

▶▶ Writing — Development of fine motor skills; correct letter formation.

The *Report of the Task Force on Dyslexia* (2002) addressed the identification of learning difficulties arising from dyslexia. This report proposed a "phased process of *assessment*" for the identification of learning difficulties arising from dyslexia. It proposed a four-phase model of assessment. The purpose of assessment at each stage is to:

▶▶ Identify the student's learning needs.

▶▶ Make necessary adjustments to teaching.

▶▶ Evaluate and record learning outcomes.

▶▶ Determine the need for further assessment and intervention. (p. 64)

At the *emergent literacy stage*, skilled teacher observation may identify a "learning difference" among children. The class teacher's response to such early indicators of possible learning difficulties may be to "notice and adjust" his/her teaching. This means differentiating the teaching according to the child's needs and monitoring the child's progress.

If observation by the child's teacher and parents indicates that pre-reading/emergent literacy skills are not developing along expected lines, the child's learning difference — a marked difference between expected and observed development — should be noted and adjustments made to instruction. If adjusted learning targets are not achieved, more formal diagnostic assessment (such as recommended above) should proceed.

Identifying Learning Difficulties

Phase 1 Initial identification of a learning difference (ages 3-5)

Phase 2 Identification of a possible learning difficulty arising from dyslexia (ages 5-7)

Phase 3 Formal identification of dyslexia and analysis of needs (ages 7-12)

Phase 4 "Annual Review of Learning Needs" (age 12+)

(Report of the Task Force on Dyslexia, 2002)

The phases of this assessment model may be viewed alongside the procedures outlined in the *Learning Support Guidelines* (DES, 2000). Each phase of the model is viewed as lying along a continuum. The suggested age ranges are approximate.

There is a broad-based correspondence across Phases 1 and 2 of this model of assessment and the emergent literacy stage.

Phases 3 and 4 of the Task Force model of assessment correspond broadly with the next stages of development as a child progresses beyond early literacy.

DIAGNOSTIC ASSESSMENT BEYOND EARLY LITERACY

For pupils who have moved beyond the early reading stages, diagnostic assessment may focus on:

▶▶ Reading accuracy

▶▶ Listening comprehension/Reading comprehension

▶▶ Sight word recognition

▶▶ Phonological awareness

▶▶ Auditory/Visual discrimination skills

▶▶ Word identification skills

▶▶ Analysis of pupil's difficulties in oral reading (miscue analysis)

- ▶▶ Reading fluency
- ▶▶ Reading rate
- ▶▶ Study skills
- ▶▶ Spelling
- ▶▶ Free writing
- ▶▶ Observational assessment (informal measures)
- ▶▶ Additional relevant information

DIFFICULTIES, DISCREPANCIES AND DIFFERENCES

A diagnostic assessment will provide information on how the child is learning and pinpoint his/her specific difficulties. It will also help the class teacher in differentiating aspects of the wider curriculum if necessary. Reid (1998) states that assessment for Specific Learning Difficulties should take note of the pupil's *difficulties*, *discrepancies* and individual pupil *differences*.

DIFFICULTIES

The child's difficulties may be noted in the area of literacy skills, numeracy skills, memory problems or oral language difficulties. Difficulties may be detected by testing the following skills:

- ▶▶ Word reading
- ▶▶ Spelling
- ▶▶ Phonological Skills
- ▶▶ Non word reading
- ▶▶ Auditory/Visual discrimination
- ▶▶ Number facts — eg addition, subtraction

Note: Consult *Drumcondra English Profiles* (Shiel, Murphy, 2000) for checklists and teaching strategies for assessing oral language development.

Discrepancies

The teacher may observe discrepancies by comparing the child's ability in areas such as reading comprehension and reading accuracy (decoding); listening comprehension and reading comprehension; oral expression and written expression. The child may have stronger ability in certain areas than others. Diagnostic testing will provide further information. Tests may include:

▶▶ Reading comprehension

▶▶ Listening comprehension

▶▶ Writing skills — informal assessment of writing portfolio

Differences

Individual differences in learning style, strengths and needs should be noted. The teacher continues to collect assessment information while teaching the student (Lerner, 1997). Information about the student's learning style can be obtained through short lessons. By careful observation, the teacher will also gain insights into how this child learns most effectively. Observational assessment would include the following factors:

▶▶ Attention/Concentration — teacher observation

▶▶ Interaction with teacher/with peers — teacher observation

▶▶ Motor skills — parent/teacher observation

▶▶ Organisational skills — parent/teacher observation

▶▶ Pupil's preferred learning style — teacher's careful observation of the above

▶▶ Self esteem; motivation; confidence — parent/teacher observation

THE INDIVIDUAL EDUCATION PLAN

- ▶▶ What is an IEP?
- ▶▶ Current Context for IEPs
- ▶▶ Planning Individual Programmes: Writing the IEP
- ▶▶ The IEP Planning Sheet (Sample)
- ▶▶ Writing the IEP Document
- ▶▶ Completed Individual Profile and Learning Programme (Sample)

WHAT IS AN IEP?

An *IEP* is an *Individual Education Plan*. It is a planning process which encourages and promotes planning and assessment for an individual child. The term IEP refers to both a *process* and a *product* or document (Tod, 2000).

- ▶▶ The *process* refers to the assessment undertaken over time and in context, along with the prioritising of aims and learning targets.
- ▶▶ The *product* or document is a summary of the aims and targets to be met, in addition to the learning outcomes expected by all involved in the IEP.

An IEP may include not only goals relating to academic or cognitive development but also those relating to motor skills, social skills, self-help skills or emotional development.

CURRENT CONTEXT FOR IEPS

BACKGROUND TO THE IEP IN IRELAND

- ▶▶ In Ireland, there is a current trend toward developing individualised education plans or programmes which address the needs of children who are experiencing serious learning difficulties. This trend comes against a background of new developments in legislation which impact upon the provision of special education services according to *need*.
- ▶▶ The *Learning Support Guidelines* (2000) recommend the use of an *Individual Profile and Learning Programme* (IPLP) for pupils receiving learning support in the context of the school's Learning Support policy.

▶▶ The proposed Special Education Council will take over the "operations" function of the Special Education Section of the Department of Education and Science in the near future. Within this context, it is proposed that "Special Needs Organisers" would "ensure the progress of students with disabilities is tracked and that it is reviewed at regular intervals". This proposal underlines the importance of maintaining appropriate records and assessment reports in relation to these students.

(A National Support Service for Special Education for Students with Disabilities, Report of Planning Group, November, 2000)

Maintaining an IEP for all pupils with identified special needs will become more and more important in the future in the context of the overall school plan.

LEGISLATION AND THE ROLE OF THE LEARNING SUPPORT TEACHER

Recent legislation in Ireland now has particular relevance to all schools, parents, teachers and children, particularly those children with special needs. New laws are coming into place whose function it is to protect all children, ensuring that their constitutional rights are protected throughout their years in school.

▶▶ The Education Act, 1998

▶▶ Equal Status Act, 2000

▶▶ Disabilities Bill, 2000

▶▶ Education Welfare Act, 2000

EDUCATION ACT, 1998

▶▶ The stated objectives of this act include: "(to) give practical effect to the constitutional rights of children, including children who have a disability or who have other special educational needs as they relate to education" (Section 6 [a], p. 10).

▶▶ Section 9 states that one of the functions of a school is to "ensure that the educational needs of all students, including those with a disability or other special educational needs, are identified and provided for" (p. 13).

▶▶ Section 21 — A School Plan: This document should include a policy statement on pupils with special needs. "The school plan shall state the objectives of the school relating to equality of access to and participation in the school and the measures which the school proposes to take to achieve those objectives, including equality of access to and participation in the school by students with disabilities or who have other special educational needs" (Section 21 [2], p. 22).

▶▶ Section 15 (2) — Enrolment policy: A Board of Management is required to publish an enrolment admission policy to include a policy for students with disability/special needs. One of the principles outlined in the Education Act is *inclusiveness*. Others are *equality*, *parental choice* and *respect*.

▶▶ Section 9 — Parental rights: The Education Act refers to the right of parents to have access to school records relating to the progress of a student.

EQUAL STATUS ACT, 2000

The aim of this Act is to promote equality and prohibit discrimination in relation to the provision of services. The discriminatory grounds include disability (Section 3). Schools can treat students with disabilities differently only if the disability is making the provision of educational services impossible for other students or having a seriously detrimental effect on that provision. If the State provides grants or aids for assisting in providing special treatment or facilities, there may be an onus on the service provider to avail of these grants.

EDUCATION WELFARE ACT, 2000

The purpose of this Act is to promote regular school attendance and to tackle the problems of absenteeism and early school leaving. A National Education Welfare Board will be established, with Education Welfare Officers employed to assist children at risk and those who experience difficulties in or out of school. These measures have not yet come into place.

DISABILITIES BILL, 2000

The National Disability Authority (NDA) was launched in 2000. This authority will advise the government on development of policy for persons with disabilities. Following this process, a Disabilities Act is expected to come into law. The main purpose of this Act will be to ensure the full participation of persons with disabilities in society, including children. The *Report of the Task Force on Autism* (2001), in its summary of legislative change in the area of disability, mentions that the NDA includes "annual individualised education plans leading to a 'contract' between school, child and parent" (p. 549) for consideration in the drafting of the new Act.

PLANNING INDIVIDUAL PROGRAMMES

WRITING THE IEP

Teachers in England and the United States have been familiar with Individual Education Plans (IEP) for many years. IEPs have been in use in England since the 1980s and in the US since the mid 1970s. With the introduction of a Code of Practice in the UK in 1994, schools have responded to the challenge of producing IEPs which "identify needs, set specific learning targets, and assist teachers in planning suitable programmes in order to meet these targets and the pupils' needs" (DfE, 1994, p. 119).

Assessment for IEP planning must be undertaken in context and over time so that appropriate targets can be set. The aim of the assessment is to inform the planning of any "different or extra" provision needed for the pupil to make progress.

In her book *Individual Education Plans and Dyslexia* (2000), Janet Tod summarises this IEP process. Tod recommends that the following questions be kept in mind when planning to write an IEP.

1.   What are the agreed areas of concern for this pupil?
2.   What are the likely long-term aims for the pupil?
3.   Under what conditions does this pupil learn most effectively? (This includes recording strengths and needs.)
4.   Which resources can be brought to bear to support pupil learning, ie parents, peers etc.? (p. 43)

INCLUSIVE CURRICULUM

Westwood (1993) states that where Individual Education Plans are required: "IEPs should indicate clearly not only what a student needs to do which is different from the rest of the class, but also the areas of the curriculum where he or she can be counted in with the others. Ideally such inclusion will be for most of the school day" (p. 5).

IEP: THE PROCESS

The IEP serves two purposes (Lerner, 1985). The first is a written plan or statement for a particular student. This plan prescribes specific educational objectives for an individual student. The second purpose is as a management tool for the entire assessment/teaching process. The IEP includes all the assessment evaluation and the teaching strategies recommended for this student.

1. Assessment for IEP planning starts with an analysis of the child's individual *strengths and needs*. The information available from screening tests administered by class teacher, diagnostic assessment tests carried out by eg the LS teacher, checklists (behaviour, oral language skills etc.) and observations by teachers and parents form the basis of information sought for an IEP.

2. *Priorities* may then be listed according to key skills: reading and spelling skills, oral language competence, mathematical ability etc.

3. *Objectives/Targets* should be brief, specific and measurable. They are concerned with medium-term planning, focussing on areas for action and details of the programme of work to be taught. They should cover the areas identified as priority needs, eg literacy, numeracy, communication (language) and behaviour/social skills.

4. *Strategies* include the particular teaching methodologies, strategies, equipment/resources used, along with named persons who will implement programmes. Detailed instructions may be specified in order to meet these targets.

Note: Objectives/Targets and Strategies (3, 4) are stated in detail in the IEP document. The *planning* is the first stage in the process. The document or *product* follows.

THE PLANNING PROCESS

PLANNING TO WRITE AN IEP

A SAMPLE

Name of Student   *Thomas D.*

Class   *5th*

Strengths

> *Very artistic. Good at drawing.*
> *Wants to please. Seeks approval from adults and other children. Seeks praise .*
> *Interested in nature.*
> *Construction/Mechanical skills good. Lego projects very good .*

Needs

> *Improve concentration and attention skills.*
> *Decrease impulsivity.*
> *Complete written tasks.*
> *Listening comprehension weak. Cannot follow verbal instructions.*
> *Constantly interrupts teacher and other pupils.*
> *Immature behaviour, not age appropriate. Poor social skills.*

Priority Needs

> *Improve attention to tasks.*
> *Improve literacy skills — reading, spelling skills and written work.*

Further Information – Questions to be answered

> *Was referral ever made for speech and language assessment?*
> *Consult with NEPS (school psychologist) re ADHD diagnosis*
> *Contact parents for information re private tutor to discuss areas of concern*
> *Checklist for oral language behaviour*

Date: *October 2002*   Signed: *Teacher*

IEP: THE PRODUCT (WRITTEN DOCUMENT)

The format of the IEP may differ from school to school, depending on how useful a particular format is considered to be. Teachers may prefer a certain style of document and may wish to design their own IEP format.

The *Code of Practice* (1994) in the UK sets out clear and specified areas to be included in an IEP. They include the following:

▶▶ The nature of the child's learning difficulty

▶▶ Action — Special needs provision

Staff involved, frequency of support

External specialists involved, including frequency and timing

Specific programmes/activities/materials and equipment

▶▶ Help from parents at home

▶▶ Targets to be achieved in a given time

▶▶ Monitoring and assessment arrangements

▶▶ Review arrangements and date

(Code of Practice 2.93)

WRITING THE IEP DOCUMENT

Based on the identified needs and areas of concern highlighted during the IEP planning stage (see Sample of IEP Planning Sheet, page 53), the LST now sets practical targets to be met and plans the teaching strategies to achieve these targets or objectives.

An instructional term of approximately 13-20 weeks is the recommended time frame according to the *Learning Support Guidelines* (DES, 2000).

SETTING TARGETS

Targets must be *specific, measurable, achievable* and *relevant* to long-term aims and objectives. They must also be *time-related*. This is called setting SMART targets (Lloyd & Berthelot, 1992).

WHAT TARGETS WILL I SET?

➤➤ Three or four targets may be set relating to each priority need identified. These needs might be in literacy, numeracy, communication or behaviour/social skills. It is important that the teacher uses the child's strengths when writing the targets.

Remember that the targets are linked to the priority needs or long-term objectives. Targets should be stated in behavioural terms. Refer to the IEP Planning Sheet (page 53) and ask the question: "What would I like this child to be able to do at the end of term which s/he cannot do now?"

➤➤ As the supplementary or "learning support" teaching usually takes place away from the classroom in a place such as the "Reading Room", the IEP target should take account of *transferring the learning* of new skills back to the classroom. This idea is central to the planning of targets as recommended in the *Learning Support Guidelines*. (See section on Reading: *Reading Recovery*, by Marie Clay).

It is important to note that pupils with identified learning *difficulties* may have a slower rate of progress in attaining automatic reading and writing skills. They will therefore need to "revisit" areas of work from the previous term.

➤➤ Set specific targets in reading, for example, which allow the child to consolidate basic sight vocabulary. The same list of 100 words may be used for two terms (see page 108). Term 1 expects the child to read the list with 60% accuracy. Term 2 aims for 100% accuracy.

➤➤ Avoid stating general targets such as "Will improve reading skills". Instead, set out the areas of literacy skills to be achieved during this term. Be realistic. You cannot expect major improvements in all areas. Make sure the targets are derived directly from the stated priority needs. State the *level* or grade of reader to be achieved. Which *word identification* skills will you and the child concentrate on this term? For example, will it be *syllabication*, reading and writing two or three syllable words? Or will you focus on *prefixes and suffixes* in an attempt to give child the strategy of finding the *root word* as a new and transferable skill?

➤➤ Targets should state who is responsible for their achievement. They may include the class teacher — "the first line of responsibility"; the LST; or the child's parent/guardian.

It should be made clear who is responsible for helping the child achieve the targets. This may be the class teacher ("the first line of responsibility"), the LST or the child's parent/guardian.

STRATEGIES

The Learning Support Teacher will decide on the teaching method(s) and the specific programmes or resources which are most appropriate to the needs of the student. The LST and the class teacher should collaborate on strategies to be used.

▶▶ For example, a teaching strategy to improve fluency and comprehension in reading could include: (a) *paired reading* to be carried out by parent for 10 minutes per night; (b) reading 1-2 pages aloud to teacher each day; (c) retelling the story s/he has just read to a small group in Reading Room.

▶▶ A specific approach may be taught for daily spelling practice, eg Look, Cover, Write, Check.

▶▶ Strategies to improve word identification skills may include: practice in breaking words into syllables; creating word families using *onsets* and *rimes*; linking phonemic awareness with phonics etc. A completed sample IEP is on page 59.

(There are more examples in Part 4: Reading, pages 89-114.)

EVALUATION — MONITORING PROGRESS

At the end of the specified time, targets will be assessed. Remember: targets should be easily "measured". *Informal* measures would be used (eg teacher observation, examining portfolio of written work), along with *criterion referenced* measures (eg testing of 100 word list; basic sight vocabulary). Assessment measures could include *formal* standardised tests (eg Neale Analysis of Reading; Drumcondra Primary Maths Test).

Some targets may not achieve 100% mastery in the given time. A range of levels and different types of measurement should therefore be included.

The IEP document should be clear and easy-to-use. It is a "working document' which should be user-friendly.

REVIEW

The student's IEP should be reviewed regularly and re-evaluated in terms of student progress. The time frame may be at the end of an instructional term or at least annually. The class teacher, LST, parents, and anybody else involved in the IEP process, should attend. Sufficient time must be set aside for this review.

It is considered good practice to involve the child himself/herself and for him/her to know what the targets are. The child is encouraged to take responsibility for his/her own progress. The review will evaluate the progress the child has made. Some targets will have been met, while others may not have been achieved. The next step in the assessment/teaching/learning process can now be planned.

In general, schools in Ireland do not have wide experience of using IEPs. Special schools are more likely to have their own individual planning process in place which addresses the individual needs of students.

However, in the interest of ensuring that additional resources and services such as special provision or learning support are most effective, the IEP process as outlined above is a valuable tool for the teacher, parent and student.

INDIVIDUAL EDUCATION PLAN
BLANK SAMPLE

TARGETS (short-term goals)

1.

2.

3

4.

STRATEGY (resources, teaching programmes)

1.

2.

3

4.

EVALUATION		DATE		
TARGET MEASUREMENT TOOL				
Observation				
Test				
Class work				
Portfolio				
Other				
TARGET	**1**	**2**	**3**	**4**
MET				
NOT MET				
HAS IMPROVED				

TARGETS (short-term goals)

1. *Writing* — To plan, edit and write a story with clear beginning, middle and end.

2. *Spelling* — To apply knowledge of visual "letter strings" to written spellings.

3. *Reading* — Will complete written cloze exercises based on assigned reading; having read a story, will retell it in sequence.

4. *Maths* — Will recite 4x times tables.

STRATEGY (resources, teaching programmes)

1. *Writing* — Teach structure by posing questions related to story ideas. Who? What? When? Where? Why?

2. *Spelling* — Work on letter string "ough" and "ear"; Follow *Alpha to Omega* program; also direct teaching of *Look, Cover, Write, Check* method. Use *Phonological Awareness Training* Program (PAT program) level 2.

3. *Reading* — Use cloze activities to help child predict, daily practice on "cloze procedure" worksheets; teach child to sequence ideas in text, to get overview. Teach *SQ3R* strategy (survey, question, read, recall, review).

4. *Maths* — Teach "doubles" and "near doubles" as strategy for multiplication by x2, x4, x8.

EVALUATION	DATE

TARGET MEASUREMENT TOOL

Observation (1) Teacher observes process of writing, editing, discussion of ideas **(3)** Teacher observes comprehension strategies used.

Test (2) Daily spelling test. **(2)** End-of-term class spelling test **(4)** Test multiplication facts weekly **(3)** End-of-Year comprehension test

Class work (2) daily dictation **(4)** daily multiplication facts test **(3)** Child self-corrects cloze activities daily.

Portfolio (1) Creative writing folder

Other

TARGET	1	2	3	4
MET				
NOT MET				
HAS IMPROVED				

A completed sample of an Individual Profile and Learning Programme (IPLP) can be seen in *Learning Support Guidelines* pp. 70,71. An example of an adapted programme follows.

INDIVIDUAL PROFILE AND LEARNING PROGRAMME

Name: *Anne*	Class: *3rd*
Address:	Class teacher:
	Learning Support teacher:
Telephone	Commencement date of supplementary teaching: *October '02*
Date of Birth:	Review date: *January '03*

Screening Assessment

Name of Test	Date	Result	Date	Result
MICRA-T	*Sept '02*	*PR 8*		

Diagnostic Assessment

Neale Analysis Form B	*Oct '02*	*Accuracy PR 8* *Comprehension PR 5*		
Marino Word Recognition Test	*Oct '02*	*7.8 years*		

Informal Assessment before Supplementary Teaching:	**Informal Assessment after Supplementary Teaching:**
100 Word List (Dolch) = ³⁰/100 *Phonological Awareness Battery (PhAB)* *Highlighted (concerns)* *Rhyme Test* *Non-Word Recognition Test*	

Summary of Other Information (For example from parents, class teacher, psychologist, speech and language therapist etc.)
- *Expressive Language Difficulty*

Learning Strengths and Attainments
- *Is motivated by success*
- *Loves listening to stories*

Priority Learning Needs
- *Increase basic sight vocabulary*
- *Improve reading accuracy*

INDIVIDUAL PROFILE AND LEARNING PROGRAMME

Learning Targets for the Period	Date Achieved
● *Read from 100 Word list with 90% accuracy* ● *Read onset-rime words* ● *Recognise rhyming words when heard* ● *Supply a rhyming word in oral cloze sentences* ● *Read Fuzzbuzz Books 1 - 12*	

Learning Support Activities — Learning Support Teacher

● *Use PAT Program, Level I — Onset and rime*
● *Sounds Abound Program — Rhyming*
● *Look-and-Say Approach to sight words. Games to reinforce:*

Materials

● *"Word Bag" for analysis of sounds*
● *Flash cards*
● *Word Bingo*
● *Phonic Bingo*
● *Ginn Language workbooks*

Learning Support Activities — Class Teacher

● *Opportunities for retelling a story, attention to sequencing*
● *Reward child's effort + eye contact*
● *Praise for staying "on task" — Use stickers etc.*
● *Written sequences to follow up words learnt with LST*

Learning Support Activities — Home

● *Paired reading with parent 7 - 10 minutes per night*

Supplementary Teaching	☐ Group	Duration of Programme from	to
	☐ Individual	Number of weeks	

Day	Monday	Tuesday	Wednesday	Thursday	Friday
Time					
Location					

REFERENCES

Department of Education (1988). *Guidelines on Remedial Education.* Dublin: The Stationery Office.

Department of Education & Employment (1994). *Code of Practice on the identification and assessment of special educational needs.* London: HMSO.

Department of Education & Science (1999). *Developing a School Plan: Guidelines for Primary Schools.* Dublin: The Stationery Office.

Department of Education & Science (2000). A National Support Service for Special Education for Students with Disabilities. *Report of Planning Group.* Dublin: The Stationery Office.

Department of Education & Science (2000). *Learning Support Guidelines.* Dublin: The Stationery Office.

Department of Education & Science (2002). Circular SP.ED 08/02. *Applications for full or part–time resource teacher support to address the special education needs of children with disabilities.* Dublin: The Stationery Office.

Government of Ireland (1998). *Education Act.* Dublin: The Stationery Office.

Lerner, J. (1997). *Learning Disabilities: Theories, Diagnosis and Teaching Strategies.* Boston: Houghton Mifflin Company.

Nugent, M. (2002). "Teachers' views of working with an individual education plan in an Irish special school". *REACH Journal of Special Needs Education in Ireland, 15* (2) 98-112.

Reid, G. (1998). *Dyslexia: A Practitioner's Handbook.* England: Wiley.

Shiel, G., & Murphy, R. (2000). *Drumcondra English Profiles: A framework for assessing oral language, reading and writing in primary schools.* Dublin: Educational Research Centre.

Task Force on Autism. (2001). *Report.* Dublin: The Stationery Office.

Task Force on Dyslexia. (2002). *Report.* Dublin: Government Publications.

Tod, J. (2000). *Individual Education Plans: Dyslexia.* London: David Fulton Publishers.

Westwood, P. (1993). *Commonsense methods for children with special needs.* London: Routledge.

THE NATIONAL EDUCATIONAL PSYCHOLOGICAL SERVICE (NEPS)

BRÍD CLANCY/NEPS

▶▶ Background

▶▶ The NEPS Mission

▶▶ The NEPS Psychologist at School Level

▶▶ Educational Psychology: An Ecologically Valid Approach

▶▶ Why refer?

▶▶ Whom to refer?

▶▶ What will the psychologist do?

▶▶ WISC-III

BACKGROUND

The National Educational Psychological Service (NEPS) was established in September 1999 as an agency of the Department of Education and Science. The *Report of the Planning Group* recommended that the agency would have an overall target of 200 psychologists, to be achieved over a five-year period. It is envisaged that all schools will have access to the NEPS service before the end of the school year 2003-2004.

(NEPS, Induction Documentation)

The NEPS Mission

...to support the personal, social and educational development of all children through the application of psychological theory and practice in education, having particular regard for children with special educational needs...

(Working Together to Make a Difference for Children, NEPS Statement of Strategy, 2001-2004)

THE NEPS PSYCHOLOGISTS AT SCHOOL LEVEL

At school level, the NEPS psychologists will be responsible for the following.

1. Engage in individual casework with students with special needs.

2. Collaborate with others in devising and evaluating appropriate interventions for such students, bearing in mind that there is a continuum of educational need within each category of disability.

3. Provide a consultancy service to teachers and parents of students with special needs.

4. Contribute to whole school planning in relation to the inclusion of children with disabilities.

5. Contribute to relevant professional development programmes for teachers.

(NEPS, 2001, p. 9)

EDUCATIONAL PSYCHOLOGY: AN ECOLOGICALLY VALID APPROACH

As a *discipline*, Educational Psychology refers to the application of psychological theory, principles and research findings to educational contexts. In order to create an *environment* which will enhance learning and development, this will involve applying a knowledge of how children develop and learn in practical ways.

In *practice*, Educational Psychology utilises theory and research from a wide range of other disciplines: education, special education, organisational psychology, clinical and counselling psychology, management.

In *reality*, a large proportion of everyday work involves working with and for children who are experiencing difficulties (eg learning difficulties, emotional and behavioural difficulties). This work may occur at one or more levels.

This means that while an individual child may be referred because s/he is not learning, the "assessment" might include the consideration of factors other than those "within the child'. This *ecologically valid* method of working moves away from the "medical model" with its notion that a child who isn't learning has "something wrong with him/her".

SCHOOL-BASED WORK IS LIKELY TO INVOLVE:

Individual Casework
Working on the case of one child

▼　　　　▼

Individual "Assessments"
Observation. Testing.
Interviewing. Counselling.
Making recommendations.
Supporting IEP Development.
Supporting parents.

Consultation
(re individuals or groups)
Working with other adults in clarifying the problem situation and generating possible solutions. This should be collaborative, with all individuals having equally-valued expertise. The psychologist is not seen as the "expert" coming with ready-made solutions.

▲　　　　▲

about 65% of school-based workload

Support & Development
Working with "systems"

▼　　　　▼

SEN/LS Policy & Practice
Discipline Policy & Practice
Pastoral Care
Bullying
Behaviour Management
Categories of LD (eg dyslexia)

Consultation
In-service Courses
Information Sessions
Parents' Talks
Project Work
Research
Setting up Cluster Groups
etc.

▲　　　　▲

about 35% of school-based workload

SEN = Special Educational Needs
LS = Learning Support

WHY REFER?

Information regarding the *referral procedure* preferred by your school psychologist should be obtained from him or her. It is always important, however, to be clear about your *reasons* for referring a child to the school psychologist and to communicate these reasons clearly. Reasons for referral might include the following.

1. Obtain further information about a particular child's strengths and weaknesses, learning style etc. in order to "fine tune" teaching or assist in developing an individualised programme for teaching and/or behaviour management.

2. Determine eligibility for extra resources (see DES *Circular 8/2002* re. resource hour allocation by "category" of learning difficulty). For students at second level, to determine eligibility for *Reasonable Accommodations in Certificate Examinations* (DES, S11/2000).

3. "Connect" a family to other support agencies (counselling, speech therapy etc.).

WHOM TO REFER?

Before referring a child to the psychologist, the school should employ an action plan similar to the following.

1. *All* teachers read the *Learning Support Guidelines*.

2. Class teachers screen all children for reading, maths and general difficulties and collate results onto database (as agreed at "whole school" level).

3. Follow flow-chart in the *Learning Support Guidelines* (p. 60) to decide which children to refer to LS teacher for diagnostic assessment.

4. When children have received at least one instructional term (preferably two) of learning support (with an Individual Profile & Learning Programme) resulting in little or no progress for no apparent reason, they may be considered for psycho-educational assessment.

5. Some children may be entitled to resource teaching hours under the terms of DES *Circulars 8/99* and *8/02*. Following initial screening, the educational psychologist should be consulted regarding these children.

If the pupil's difficulties are markedly unresponsive to supplementary teaching, consideration should be given, in consultation with the pupil's parents, to referring the child for psychological assessment. Such an assessment would provide additional information and advice to the school on drawing up an appropriate learning programme for the pupil. It would also allow for the possibility of providing resource-teacher support or other special educational support for the pupil, as appropriate.

(Learning Support Guidelines, DES 2002, p. 65)

WHAT WILL THE PSYCHOLOGIST DO?

▶▶ Observe the child in class and/or in the yard. *and/or*

▶▶ Administer a range of individual assessment instruments. These may include a psychometric test of cognitive "abilities" (or IQ test), tests of attainment, self-esteem inventories). *and/or*

▶▶ Give rating scales (behaviour, social skills) to teachers and/or parents to complete. *and/or*

▶▶ Conduct interviews. *and/or*

▶▶ Use sociograms.

▶▶ Consult with relevant adults.

THE WECSHLER INTELLIGENCE SCALE FOR CHILDREN, THIRD EDITION UK (WISC-III)

The most commonly used individual psychometric test is the *Wecshler Intelligence Scale for Children*, Third Edition*UK *(WISC-III* UK*)*. This is an individual test which uses 13 subtests (most psychologists use between 10 and 12 of these subtests) to obtain the following:

▶▶ an overall *Fullscale IQ* ("Intelligence Quotient") (Mean: 100; Standard Deviation:15)

▶▶ a *Verbal IQ* score (Mean: 100; SD:15)

▶▶ a *Performance* (non-verbal) *IQ* score (Mean: 100; SD:15)

▶▶ Four "Index" scores (Mean: 100; SD:15)

* Note: This is a restricted test which can only be purchased and used by registered educational and clinical psychologists.

1. *Verbal Comprehension* — Verbal knowledge and comprehension retained from formal education which reflect application of verbal skills in new situations. Includes: general knowledge, verbal concept formation, auditory memory, "common sense", vocabulary, mental maths.

2. *Perceptual Organisation* — Perceptual and organisational skills reflecting ability to interpret and/or organise visually perceived material. Includes: visual memory, visual sequencing, non-verbal inductive and deductive reasoning, visuo-motor coordination.

3. *Freedom from Distractibility* — Ability to attend to and concentrate on verbal-auditory tasks which place demands on short-term memory and which are easily influenced by environmental distractions.

4. *Processing Speed* — Speed of mental and motor processing.

    ▸▸ Up to 13 "scaled scores" for the 13 *subtests* (Mean: 10; SD:3).

    ▸▸ Ipsative (innate) "strengths" and "weaknesses" obtained by "clustering" the 13 scaled scores. This will elicit "hypotheses" or theories regarding the child's memory, perceptual skills, reasoning and many other cognitive abilities. These theories must be corroborated by information from other sources.

Psychologists usually only report a "category" or "range" for IQs and Index scores. Other than the Fullscale IQ which is always reported, only noteworthy fluctuations (ie those which are statistically significant) which indicate specific "strengths" and "weaknesses" will be reported. Schools should discuss these with their psychologist and try to establish implications for the child's learning programme.

Remember that a child's performance on a *WISC* may vary over time. Predictions about a child's "potential" should never be made on the basis of a single IQ score. Indeed, such tests have not gone uncriticised and many psychologists use equally valid methodologies which do not involve the administration of IQ tests.

REFERENCES

Department of Education & Science (1998). *A National Educational Psychological Service: Report of the Planning Group*. Dublin: the Stationery Office.

Department of Education & Science (1999). *Developing a School Plan: Guidelines for Primary Schools*. Dublin: The Stationery Office.

Department of Education & Science (2000). Circular S11/2000: *Report of the expert advisory group on certificate examinations in relation to arrangements for the assessment of candidates with special needs in Certificate Examinations*. Dublin: The Stationery Office.

Department of Education & Science (2000). *Learning Support Guidelines*. Dublin: The Stationery Office.

Department of Education & Science (2002). Circular SPED 08/02. *Applications for full or part-time resource teacher support to address the special education needs of children with disabilities*.

National Educational Psychological Service (NEPS). (2001). *NEPS Statement of Strategy, 2000-2004: Working Together to Make a Difference for Children*. Dublin: The Stationery Office.

Weschler Intelligence Scale for Children, Third Edition UK (WISC III). Restricted tests which can only be purchased and used by registered educational and clinical psychologists.

PART 3

DYSLEXIA — IDENTIFICATION, ASSESSMENT AND SUPPORT

DYSLEXIA IN IRELAND

Educational systems often define dyslexia as a *specific learning difficulty affecting reading, spelling or writing.*

In Ireland, the Special Education Review Committee (Dublin, 1993) used the term "specific learning *disability*" instead of *dyslexia* or *specific learning difficulty*. The Committee defined the disability as "impairment in specific aspects of reading, writing and arithmetical notation, the primary cause of which is not attributable to assessed ability being below the average range, to defective sight or hearing, emotional factors, a physical condition, or to any extrinsic adverse circumstances" (p. 86).

This is an "exclusionary" definition of dyslexia. It states what dyslexia is *not* but does not explain what it *is* or how it affects the child.

In 1999, the then Minister for Education, Dr Michael Woods, used the term "dyslexia" to identify that group of children as described by the *SERC Report*. The following year, he set up a task force on dyslexia to "review the current range of educational provision and support services available to children with specific reading disability in Ireland" (Task Force on Dyslexia, 2002, p. xi)

The Task Force proposed a broader concept of the term dyslexia, describing it in its final draft report as a "continuum of specific learning difficulties…". The Task Force states:

> *Dyslexia is a continuum of specific learning difficulties manifested by problems in acquiring one or more basic skills (reading, spelling, writing, number), such problems being unexpected in relation to other abilities. Dyslexic difficulties can be described at the neurological, cognitive and behavioural levels. They are typically characterised by inefficient information processing, including difficulties in phonological processing, working memory, rapid naming and automaticity of basic skills. Difficulties in organisation, sequencing and motor skills may also be present. Dyslexia may be associated with early spoken language difficulties.*
>
> (*Report of the Task Force on Dyslexia, 2002, p. 31*)

The Task Force also recognises that the learning difficulties arising from dyslexia:

▶▶ occur across the lifespan and may manifest themselves in different ways at different ages

▶▶ may co-exist with difficulties in the area of number

▶▶ may be associated with early spoken language difficulties

▶▶ may be alleviated by appropriate intervention

▶▶ increase or reduce in severity, depending on environmental factors

▶▶ occur in all socio-economic circumstances

▶▶ coexist with other learning difficulties such as Attention Deficit Disorder (ADD), and may or may not represent a primary difficulty

(*Report of Task Force on Dyslexia*, 2002, p. 31)

Note: The terms *specific reading disability* and *specific reading difficulty* are both used in the literature on reading difficulties. In Ireland and the USA, *specific reading disability* is widely used (see *SERC Report*), whereas in Northern Ireland and the UK, *specific reading difficulty* is used. Both terms include dyslexia.

DEFINITIONS OF DYSLEXIA

There is a high interest in dyslexia among parents, teachers and the media. Over the past number of years, there has been considerable research into its "causes" and "cures", with many suggested methods and interventions, both teaching and non-teaching. There has also been a tendency for definitions to describe the difficulties encountered by people with dyslexia, or to concentrate on the causes of the condition.

The following selected definitions are but a sample of accepted definitions currently in use. There is, however, no agreement on a single definition.

"Dyslexia is a combination of abilities and difficulties which affect the learning process in one or more areas of reading, spelling and writing. Accompanying weaknesses may also be seen in speed of processing, short-term memory, sequencing, auditory and/or visual perception, spoken language and motor skills."

(British Dyslexia Association, 2000)

"Dyslexia is one of several distinct learning difficulties. It is a specific language-based disorder of constitutional origin characterised by *difficulties in single-word decoding,* usually reflecting *insufficient phonological processing abilities*. These difficulties in single-word decoding are often *unexpected* in relation to age and other cognitive and academic abilities; they are not the result of generalised developmental disability or sensory impairment. Dyslexia is manifest by variable difficulty with different forms of language, often including, in addition to problems with reading, a conspicuous problem with acquiring proficiency in writing and spelling."

(Orton Dyslexia Society Research Committee, 1994)

"Dyslexia is evident when accurate and fluent word reading and/or spelling develop very incompletely or with great difficulty. This focuses on literacy learning at the "word level" and implies that the problem is severe and persistent despite appropriate learning opportunities. It provides the basis for a staged process of assessment through teaching."

(British Psychological Society, 1999, p. 12)

"Specific Learning Difficulties/Dyslexia can be identified as distinctive patterns of difficulties relating to the processing of information within a continuum from very mild to extremely severe, which result in restrictions in literacy development and discrepancies in performance within the curriculum."

(Reid, 1998, p. 2)

THEORETICAL EXPLANATIONS OF DYSLEXIA

Dyslexia is frequently described and explained in the literature at different levels: biological, cognitive and behavioural.

BIOLOGICAL LEVEL

▶▶ *Right Hemisphere Preference*: Child may display strengths in visual spatial awareness which is a "right hemisphere" skill. Child may have weakness in "left hemisphere" activities, ie skills involving language, symbols, reading.

▶▶ *Inhibited Primary Reflexes*: Recent research has shown that children with inhibited primary reflexes display more specific learning difficulties than other children. Neuro-developmental Therapy and Primary Movement exercises are based on this explanation.

▶▶ *Genetic Chromosome Research*: Research into the genetic basis of dyslexia has isolated Chromosomes 6 and 15. Scientists have found that certain clusters of genes similar to auto-immune disease (hay fever, asthma, light sensitivity) indicate a genetic cause for dyslexia.

▶▶ *Magnetic Resonance Imaging — the "Dyslexic Brain":* Studies have shown that the brain of a person with dyslexia is different from that of a person without dyslexia.

▶▶ *Inherited Disorder — family history of similar problems*: It is widely believed that there is a genetic disposition to dyslexia and that it is inheritable.

COGNITIVE LEVEL

▶▶ *Working Memory — a universal difficulty*: Parents realise that the child "…learns it one day, forgets it the next". (Adults say: "I cannot trust my memory.") These difficulties can include problems in remembering letter/sound associations which will affect the acquisition of phonics. Memory problems may also cause difficulties in retaining the meaning of a text.

▶▶ *Phonological Processing Difficulty* — breaking sounds into component parts. Phonological processing difficulties are seen in the majority of children with dyslexia. Unfamiliar words are frequently misread and this, in turn, affects comprehension.

▸▸ *Speed of Processing*: Child requires more time in class to process instructions, new information, directions etc.

▸▸ *Visual Processing Difficulties*: Poor visualising skills leading to spelling difficulties; weak visual memory.

▸▸ *Automaticity*: Reading fluency requires automatic word recognition and speed of processing. The child may have difficulty while concentrating on decoding and content at the same time.

BEHAVIOURAL LEVEL

▸▸ Speech and Language Difficulties — difficulty pronouncing multi-syllable words

▸▸ Pattern of errors in reading and spelling

▸▸ Difficulties with rote learning

▸▸ Sequencing Difficulties — eg days of week, months of year

▸▸ Poor concentration

▸▸ Organisational/time-management factors

▸▸ Unusual pattern of skills — The child is often very good orally, but has difficulty with written language, both written language and text.

▸▸ Left-Right confusion

▸▸ Self-esteem may be affected due to cycle of failure

INDICATORS OF DIFFICULTIES

In the Irish context, the *Report of the Task Force on Dyslexia (2002)* has provided guidelines to aid the identification and assessment of learning difficulties arising from dyslexia. The Task Force outlined the following list of difficulties (pp. 120-122).

INDICATORS OF A POSSIBLE LEARNING DIFFICULTY
ARISING FROM DYSLEXIA (AGES 5-7 YEARS+)

Many of these indicators may also be noted in students with other learning difficulties.

▶▶ Is slow to learn the connection between letters and sounds (alphabetic principle)

▶▶ Has difficulty separating words into sounds, and blending sounds to form words (phonemic awareness)

▶▶ Has difficulty repeating multi-syllabic words (eg *emeny* for *enemy*; *pasghetti* for *spaghetti*)

▶▶ Has difficulty decoding single words (reading single words in isolation)

▶▶ Has poor word-attack skills, especially for new words

▶▶ Confuses small or "easy" words: (eg *at/to; said/and; does/goes*)

▶▶ May make constant reading and spelling errors including:

　▶▶ Letter reversals (eg *d* for *b* as in *dog* for *bog*)

　▶▶ Letter inversions (eg *m* for *w*)

　▶▶ Letter transpositions (eg *felt* and *left*)

　▶▶ Word reversals (eg *tip* for *pit*)

　▶▶ Word substitutions (eg *house* for *home*)

▶▶ Reads slowly with little expression or fluency (oral reading is slow and laborious)

▶▶ Has more difficulty with function words (eg *is, to, of*) than with content words (eg *cloud, run, yellow*)

▶▶ May be slow to learn new skills, relying heavily on memorising without understanding

▶▶ Reading comprehension is below expectation due to poor accuracy, fluency and speed

▶▶ Reading comprehension is better than single-word reading

▶▶ Listening comprehension is better than reading comprehension

▶▶ Has trouble learning facts

▶▶ Has difficulty planning or organising

▶▶ Uses awkward pencil grip

▶▶ Has slow and poor-quality handwriting

▶▶ Has trouble learning to tell the time on an analogue clock or watch

▶▶ Has poor fine motor coordination

INDICATORS OF A POSSIBLE LEARNING DIFFICULTY
ARISING FROM DYSLEXIA (AGES 7-12 YEARS+)

Many of these indicators may also be noted in students with other learning difficulties.

▶▶ Has continued difficulty reading text aloud or silently

▶▶ Reading achievement is below expectation

▶▶ Still confuses letter sequences (eg *soiled* for *solid*; *left* for *felt*)

▶▶ Is slow at discerning and learning prefixes, suffixes, root words and other morphemes as part of reading and spelling strategies

▶▶ Poor reading accuracy, fluency, or speed interferes with reading comprehension

▶▶ Spelling is inappropriate for age and general ability (eg spelling the same word differently on the same page, use of bizarre spelling patterns, frequent letter omissions, additions and transposition)

▶▶ Poor spelling contributes to poor written expression (eg may avoid use of unfamiliar words)

▶▶ Uses avoidance tactics when asked to read orally or write

▶▶ Experiences language-related problems in maths (eg when reading word problems and directions, confuses numbers and symbols)

▶▶ Is unable to learn multiplication tables by rote

▶▶ Still confuses some directional words (eg left and right)

▶▶ Has slow or poor recall of facts

▶▶ Lacks understanding of other people's body language and facial expressions

▶▶ Has trouble with non-literal or figurative language (eg idioms, proverbs)

▶▶ Forgets to bring in or hand in homework

▶▶ Has difficulty remembering what day or month it is

▶▶ Has difficulty remembering his/her own telephone number or birthday

▶▶ Has poor planning and organisational skills

▶▶ Has poor time management

▶▶ Lacks self-confidence and has a poor self-image

SCREENING TESTS

When deciding to use a screening test for dyslexia, remember that each screening test begins from a particular view or definition of dyslexia. Screening tests may differ from each other in terms of which skills are tested.

Research is continuing in Trinity College Dublin to develop an early dyslexia screening test for use in schools in Ireland.

Samples of existing dyslexia screening tests include the following:

▶▶ Horne, J.K., Singleton, C.H., & Thomas, K.V. (1999). *LASS 11-15*. Beverley, East Yorks: Lucid Creative Ltd. (computer software and teachers manual).

▶▶ Miles, T. R. (1993). *The Bangor Dyslexia Test*. All ages. Learning Development Aids, Wisbech.

▶▶ Nicolson, R. & Fawcett, A. (1996). *Dyslexia Screening Test (DST): Age 6.6–16 years*. London: The Psychological Corporation.

For younger children aged 5-7, an individualised diagnostic assessment is more informative for the LST. Some recommended diagnostic tests may include the following:

▶▶ Hannavy, S. (1993). *Middle Infant Screening Test and Forward Together Programme (MIST)* Age 5 – 6 years. Windsor: NFER Nelson.

▶▶ Robertson, A., Fisher, J., Henderson, A. & Gibson, M. (1995). *Quest: Screening Diagnostic and Remediation Kit* (2nd ed.). Age 6 – 8+ years. Leeds: Arnold & Wheaton.

▶▶ Singleton, C.,Thomas, K. & Leedale, R. (1996). *Cognitive Profiling System (COPS), age 4 – 8 years*. Beverley, East Yorks: Lucid Creative Ltd.

▶▶ Spelman, B., & McHugh, B., (1994). *Belfield Infant Assessment Profile*. Age 4 – 7 years. Dublin: Folens.

FORMAL DIAGNOSIS OF DYSLEXIA

The Task Force recommended a *staged model of assessment* which sets out four phases or stages in identifying learning difficulties which may lead to a formal diagnosis of dyslexia. Please refer to the *Report of the Task Force on Dyslexia* for further elaboration on the formal diagnosis of dyslexia. The following is a brief summary of this model (pp. 76-77 of the *Task Force Report*).

IDENTIFYING LEARNING DIFFICULTIES ARISING FROM DYSLEXIA

TABLE 5-5

CONTINUUM OF IDENTIFICATION AND PROVISION

Phase	Procedure	Main Persons Involved	Outcomes
1. Initial Identification of a Learning Difference (Ages 3-5: Pre-school /Junior Infants)	Informal assessment by care-giver / teacher; Input from parents; Identification of a marked learning difference	Child, Principal Teacher, Care-giver, Class Teacher, Parents / Guardians	Response to learning differences within child's own class; 'Noticing and adjusting'. Some differentiation of instruction; Recording of child's response to adjustments.
2. Identification of a Possible Learning Difficulty Arising from Dyslexia (Ages 5-7+: Infants /First Class)	Formal and informal assessment; Diagnostic assessment to determine seriousness and persistence of student's learning difficulties; Review of progress through regular assessment.	Student, Principal Teacher, Class Teacher, Learning-Support Teacher; Parents / Guardians Educational Psychologist (for guidance and advice as needed).	Identification of students who are at risk of developing learning difficulties arising from dyslexia; Provision of individual or small-group differentiated instruction by Class / Learning Support Teachers; Development and implementation of Individual Learning Programme and monitoring of outcomes, as per the Learning Support Guidelines.

Note: The Model is intended to represent a continuum, with movement to the next phase (or back to an earlier phase) contingent on the student's progress in attaining targets that have been set.

Task Force on Dyslexia (2002). *Report*. Dublin: Government Publications (pp. 76-77)

CONTINUUM OF IDENTIFICATION AND SUPPORT
TABLE 5-5

Phase	Procedure	Main Persons Involved	Outcomes
3. Identification of Dyslexia and Analysis of Learning Needs (Ages: 7–12 years +: (Second-Sixth Class)	Gathering of assessment information; Multi-disciplinary review of child's difficulties and educational needs	Student, Principal Teacher, Class Teacher, Learning Support Teacher, Resource Teacher, Educational Psychologist (Assessment and advice) Parents / Guardians	Statement on degree of severity of learning difficulties arising from dyslexia; Development of an Individual Learning Programme; Provision of intensive differentiated instruction in an appropriate setting depending on level of need (provision by resource teacher in own school, enrolment in a special class or school for students with specific learning disabilities). Consideration of need for special education services determined.
4. Annual Review of Learning Needs (12 years +)	Liaison with feeder primary school: Gathering of assessment information; Multi-disciplinary review of progress and learning needs.	Multi-disciplinary Review Team including, for example, Year Head, Learning Support Teacher, Parents, Educational Psychologist (if necessary), Advocate (if desired), Guidance Counsellor.	Initial review of needs and annual review of progress based on available evidence; Consideration of severity of student's learning difficulties; development of individual learning programme, addressing, where relevant, need for assistive technology, exemption from study of Irish, and recommendations with regard to accommodations in State examinations.

LIKELY STRENGTHS AND TALENTS OF CHILDREN WHO ARE DYSLEXIC

Children will compensate for their difficulties in achieving literacy skills by expressing strengths in other areas. Teachers and parents should be aware of these strengths. The educational system lays a heavy emphasis on written expression, but children should be encouraged to display their knowledge and skills in other ways — orally, through diagrams, mind maps, or by using computer skills.

Children with dyslexia are likely to exhibit skills in the following areas:

▶▶ *Visual thinking skills* — necessary for Design and Technology; good spatial ability

▶▶ *Visual-based and multi-dimensional skills* — Art, Sculpture, Design, Architecture, Engineering

▶▶ *Entrepreneur skills* — Computer skills; good comprehension

▶▶ *Creative talents* — Original ideas expressed orally, through diagrams, or on computer

▶▶ *Future careers* may include architect, engineer, draughtsperson, computer programmers, fashion, design, broadcasting and the arts.

In class, many of these strengths are often masked by the expectation to express them through writing. Teachers should look for skills in practical subjects, original ideas as expressed orally or on computer, and for creative talent.

> *We ought to begin to pay less attention to getting everyone over the same hill using the same path. We may wish to encourage some to take different routes to the same end. Then we might see good reasons for paying careful attention to their descriptions of what they have found. We may wish to follow them some day.*
>
> (West, 1997)

SPECIALIST TEACHING OF CHILDREN WITH DYSLEXIC-TYPE DIFFICULTIES

Dyslexia cannot be "cured". With the right teaching approach, however, it can be managed so that it does not become a "life-threatening" condition.

Teachers who work with children who are dyslexic believe that the most effective teaching practices benefit not only those children with learning difficulties but in fact all children. This type of teaching should be:

▶▶ **Multi-sensory**

Multi-sensory methods can work for all children but are particularly effective with many children who are dyslexic. The teacher uses visual, aural, tactile and kinaesthetic ways to integrate the learning. The child's preferred learning style and his/her strengths give the teacher important information in designing the lesson.

▶▶ **Structured**

The work presented must be very well structured, planned and presented sequentially. The child needs to achieve success at every stage. New information should be presented in a step-by-step manner, not all at once.

▶▶ **Cumulative**

Concepts must build upon what has gone before. The child needs to activate prior knowledge to reinforce learning. Do not assume that the child will know something which has not been taught specifically. Children with dyslexia may not absorb or catch on as other children do. Check and re-check!

▶▶ **Reinforced through Practice**

Because of memory difficulties, each step must be thoroughly practised to become embedded and increase automaticity, eg in word recognition/spelling patterns etc. The child needs many different ways of reinforcing the same skill. Games are powerful motivators. Repetition and reinforcement will compensate for a child's weak memory.

▶▶ **Phonics Oriented**

Teaching needs to concentrate on phonic skills, an area which is generally weak for dyslexic children. Work in this area is always relevant to school work and will transfer to improvement in other school subjects. However, if the child is weak in phonics, the teacher should be mindful of his/her other strengths.

▶▶ **Confidence Building**

Give plenty of encouragement and praise. The child should be praised for his/her *effort* rather than the *results*. Build a good relationship with the child. Get to know him/her and find out about his/her interests. Concentrate on the individual pupil and discover ways in which you can motivate him/her.

THE DYSLEXIA-FRIENDLY SCHOOL

A whole school policy of learning support should take into account that there may be children in every class with varying degrees of learning difficulties. These difficulties can range from the mild end of the continuum to the severe.

In its policy, each school must outline how difficulties arising from dyslexia will be addressed.

By fostering a whole school approach to helping these children, the other children will benefit too.

Strategies for making your school "dyslexia friendly" may include:

▶▶ *Paired Reading* — When such a scheme is used throughout the school, it can be very effective. Parent involvement is particularly important for those children who are having difficulty in developing independent reading skills.

▶▶ *Paired Reading between Classes* — Paired Reading may be incorporated into classroom activities. Children from a senior class can become "reading partners" to younger children.

▶▶ *Whole School Behaviour Policy* — A positive behaviour policy which rewards children for effort, not just results. For example, *The Discipline for Learning* (DFL) system is gaining in popularity among schools in this regard.

▶▶ *Choice of Materials* — Choose worksheets and books with dyslexic difficulties in mind. The design of any material should be easily legible and user friendly.

▶▶ *Colour-coding* — Encourage the general use of folders, colour-coded files, coloured plastic pockets etc. as aids to children who find it difficult to organise the equipment, books, copies which they need for each subject.

▶▶ *Eye Sensitivity* — Acknowledge the possibility of eye sensitivity caused by the glare from white paper. Use cream, buff or blue worksheets where possible.

▶▶ *Child's Use of Colour* — Encourage children to use colour when presenting written work. Coloured pens and markers should be readily available.

▶▶ *Visual Stimuli* — Use pictures, sketches, diagrams to represent information. Pictures of mnemonics such as **A**ngry **E**lephants **I**n **O**range **U**nderpants (vowels) encourage children to create their own mnemonics as memory aids.

▶▶ *School Notices* — Be aware of how notices are presented around the school. Do not use block capitals. Be consistent with writing style and letters used. Joined (cursive) writing is considered "easier". Colour-coded notices are also helpful.

▶▶ *Use of Joined Writing* — There should be an overall school policy about when to introduce joined writing. There should be an agreement on writing style which is to be followed throughout the school

▶▶ *Text Fonts* — Text printed in the font "Comic Sans" may be easier to read on items such as teaching worksheets.

▶▶ *Information Technology* — All children should have access to IT, with priority given to word processing skills.

▶▶ *Word Walls* — Encourage use of "Word Walls" in all classrooms — essential 200 word list; subject words; topic words etc.

▶▶ *Word Families* — Each classroom should display: lists of word families; onset and rime lists; list of frequently used irregular words; phonic checklists.

▶▶ *School Library* — Every school library should be dyslexia-aware and should stock large print books as well as cassette tapes.

▶▶ *Parental Support* — Foster parental support by having advisory sessions about the Revised Curriculum and any changes in emphasis in literacy (English reading, oral language etc.) and numeracy (use of concrete materials in school and at home in developing concepts). There should also be a particular emphasis on how to help children with homework.

TEACHING PROGRAMMES RECOMMENDED FOR CHILDREN WHO ARE DYSLEXIC

This is not a prescriptive list but a selection of teaching programmes this author has found effective and useful.

▶▶ **A New Approach to Phonics**

Phonological Awareness Training Programme (PAT Programme). Wilson, J., (1993). Educational Psychologists Publishing. London: University College.

▶▶ **Alpha-to-Omega: The A-Z of Teaching Reading, Writing and Spelling**

Hornsby, B. & Shear, F. (1994). London: Heinemann Educational.

▶▶ **Alpha to Omega Activity Packs Stage 1,2 and 3**

Hornsby, B., & Pool, J. (1989). London: Heinemann Educational.

▶▶ **Bangor Dyslexia Teaching System (2nd ed)**

Miles, E., (1992). London: Whurr Publishers.

▶▶ **Helping Children with Reading and Spelling: A Special Needs Manual**

Reason, R., & Boote R. (1994). London: Routledge.

▶▶ **Sounds Abound: Listening, Rhyming and Reading**

Catts, H., & Olsen, T. (1993). Illinois: Linguisystems Inc.

▶▶ **Sound Linkage**

An Integrated programme for overcoming reading difficulties. Hatcher, P. (2000). London: Whurr.

▶▶ **Toe by Toe**

Highly structured multisensory reading manual for teachers and parents. Good for older children. Cowling, K., & Cowling, H., (1999). Yorks: Author.

▶▶ **Units of Sound**

Multimedia Includes CD-ROMs, tapes, books and manual. Bramly, W. (1992). Middlesex, England: Dyslexia Institute.

REFERENCES

British Psychological Society (1999). *Dyslexia, Literacy and Psychological Assessment*. Leicester.

Department of Education & Science (2000). *Learning Support Guidelines*. Dublin: The Stationery Office.

Discipline for Learning: In-service Programme for Schools (1996) Somerset: Discipline for Learning Ltd.

Johnson, M., & Peer, L. (2002). *British Dyslexia Association Handbook*. Berkshire, UK: British Dyslexia Association.

McCormack, W. (1998). *Lost for Words: Dyslexia at second level and beyond*. Dublin: Tower Press.

Ott, P. (1997). *How to detect and manage dyslexia: A reference and resource manual*. Oxford: Heinemann.

Reid, G. (1998). *Dyslexia: A Practitioner's Handbook*. England: Wiley.

Special Education Review Committee (1993). *Report*. Dublin: The Stationery Office.

Task Force on Dyslexia (2002). Report. Dublin: The Stationery Office.

West, T. G. (1991, second edition 1997) *In the Mind's Eye. Visual Thinkers, Gifted People with Learning Difficulties, Computer Images and the Ironies of Creativity*. Buffalo, N.Y.: Prometheus Books.

PART 4

READING

INTRODUCTION

All children learn to read best where certain conditions are present in their learning environment. In 2001, the National Reading Initiative commissioned a video and booklet to assist teachers in the implementation of the *Primary School Curriculum: English Language*, with particular reference to the teaching of reading. The video shows how the teaching approaches recommended can be adopted. The following is a short summary of the conditions under which children will learn best.

▸▸ The child is exposed to all kinds of books: picture books, fiction, non-fiction.

▸▸ All senses are involved in an integrated way: listening, speaking, reading and writing.

▸▸ Oral language development is encouraged by listening to rhymes, songs, listening to each other talking about books, sharing and enjoying books.

▸▸ The classroom becomes a print-rich environment with labels, signs, captions and real writing on display.

▸▸ Writing is linked with reading. With guidance from the teacher, children can create their own book(s) using words they know. This makes the experience real — real writing and real reading in which the children become engaged as readers and writers.

▸▸ There is a partnership with parents. Regular communication with parents regarding the rationale of reading instruction in the school and the involvement of parents in supporting the reading process is a vital part of this three-way partnership of Teacher-(School)-Parents-Pupils.

(National Reading Initiative, 2001)

Children with delays and difficulties in learning to read have an even greater need to experience these positive factors. They require a more concentrated and structured approach to ensure that they are given opportunities to unlock their potential.

HOW DO GOOD READERS READ?

By looking at the way in which good readers read, we may be able to discover the strategies they use.

1. They have good *phonological skills*.

2. They use *decoding strategies*.

3. They recognise words from *previous experience*.

4. They use *context clues*.

1.   PHONOLOGICAL AWARENESS

Phonological awareness means an awareness of the sounds in words and an ability to manipulate these sounds orally, to segment sounds, and to break words into syllables. Phonological awareness is now recognised as a clear predictor of a child's development in learning to read. A child with good phonological skills will have fewer difficulties when encountering new or unfamiliar texts.

LEVEL 1

At this basic level, phonological awareness involves breaking words into syllables.

Example

wig/wam   car/pet   cook/er

At this level, children will find syllabic segmentation quite easy.

LEVEL 2

This involves using *onset and rime* to manipulate sounds. These terms are used to describe the two parts of single-syllable words. The first sound is called the onset; the end sound is the rime.

Example

p/ig   fr/og   ch/imp

If a child is familiar with this approach, it will be much easier to make analogies to other words with similar "rimes". In other words, the child who can distinguish **s/ay** can read and write:

m/ay d/ay p/ay b/ay h/ay w/ay

Likewise, the child who can separate the sounds in **st/and** will know:

b/and   h/and   l/and

This is called *analogous reasoning*. It encourages the transfer of learning and lessens the memory load for children who may have memory difficulties.

LEVEL 3

Phonemic segmentation and blending is the final level of phonological awareness. This is an awareness of the individual sounds in words.

Example: When hearing the sounds of a word pronounced separately, the child will be able to blend those sounds and say the word.

u-p = up   m-a-n = man

Children who experience difficulty in learning to recognise words and in developing a sight vocabulary may also have difficulty in separating the individual sounds in words. Children with auditory processing difficulties may not find *sounding out* the individual phonemes in a word too difficult — it is *blending* the sounds together which creates the problem. However, good teaching will use the child's strengths to develop an individual approach to developing the child's potential to read fluently.

The use of large format books or "Big Books" is a very successful approach in familiarising children with rhymes, sound patterns and making analogies to other words. The text is enlarged so that the whole group can see it, read it, re-read it and discuss it. Consequently, the language activities and the listening and speaking experiences become a natural part of reading and writing. The *Primary School Curriculum, English Language Teacher Guidelines* (1999), emphasises the importance of the child's general language experience as a prerequisite for reading. Oral language activities have a central part in preparing the child to read.

Note: Large-format books are not just confined to Junior Infants. Excerpts of novels, plays, poems and well-known classics are available in Big Book format for older age groups.

2. DECODING STRATEGIES

Decoding strategies such as the following may be used by good readers. They may be based on their *phonological awareness* (an awareness of the sounds of spoken language) or by applying *word attack skills* already learnt.

▶▶ Phoneme-by-phoneme — /m/ /a/ /n/

▶▶ Onset and rime — /r/est/   /m/ug/   /sh/ip/

(The beginning part is called the *onset* and the group of letters in the end part, including the vowel, is the *rime*.)

▶▶ Segment by syllables — rab / bit

▶▶ Good readers may recognise root words, prefixes and suffixes.

form form er   in *form* er   de *form*   per *form* ing

▶▶ The good reader can apply simple *structural analysis* to a word by recognising a root word or finding a small word within the bigger word.

3. PREVIOUS EXPERIENCE

Good readers will recognise words from previous experience. It is here that a structured oral language programme which develops and expands the children's receptive language vocabulary contributes greatly to developing reading. Talking about books, discussing characters, story lines, sharing the best part, "my favourite part" etc. — all of these build a store of words to be drawn upon in future reading experiences.

4. CONTEXTUAL CLUES

Good readers use *contextual clues*. When the child is actively involved in reading and responding to text, s/he is using the *context* to give more meaning to the reading. Pictures, diagrams, sketches, details in the book all provide "cues" and "clues" to reading. A good reader extracts meaning from the text by interacting with it.

TEACHING THE CHILD WITH SPECIFIC LEARNING DIFFICULTIES

Children with specific learning disabilities or dyslexic-type reading difficulties do not necessarily require instructional strategies for learning to read which are "different" from those methods used in mainstream classrooms. What these children need is a more structured and concentrated approach to the teaching of reading. The LST has in her/his repertoire a variety of methods of instruction in reading. These methods range from the *whole language approach* or *top-down approach* using real books, to the *bottom-up approach* which emphasises phonics and begins with pupils learning letter sounds and names.

Put simply, the *top-down approach* begins with providing a variety of good literature for the children, along with reading to them every day and encouraging lots of silent reading. This approach recognises language development as part of the reading process, along with discussing books and sharing books. In this way, children learn to read *as* they read.

The *bottom-up approach*, on the other hand, begins with teaching skills such as letter/sound associations, structured phonics, word attack skills and the use of controlled text (ie only introducing those words that have already been taught).

It is recommended that you take some elements from each approach. Teaching phonics only, without exposure to a variety of good books, is not recommended. On the other hand, exposure to good books without being taught how to "decode" is not enough.

The effective teacher will incorporate elements of each approach in his/her teaching and, where necessary, will adapt an approach to meet the individual needs of a child.

READING METHODS

Language Experience Approach: The child's own words form the basis of material to be read. Child dictates a sentence… the teacher writes it down… child learns to read his/her own sentences.

Phonic Method: The child is taught the individual letter sounds, sometimes the letter name and sound simultaneously, and uses this knowledge to decode a word.

Look-and-Say Method: The pupil is shown a flash card of a complete word which s/he memorises to build up a sight vocabulary.

Multisensory Method: The child is taught to look, say, hear and feel letters and sounds simultaneously.

PAIRED READING AND SHARED READING

Strategies such as *paired reading* or *shared reading* are not methods in the strict sense. They are complementary strategies which are very effective in improving fluency in reading by providing regular practice in reading with an adult.

Paired reading involves the parent/adult and child reading together. It has become popular in schools over the last few years and is a very effective way to improve children's reading fluency and comprehension. The adult adjusts the pace of the reading to suit the child. This situation may continue for a number of weeks (five or six).

1. The child chooses the book and decides when and for how long s/he will read with the parent/adult. Seven to ten minutes per night is sufficient. Regular and consistent paired reading will enhance the progress of the weak reader.

2. Parent and child sit side-by-side and read aloud together. After a while, the child uses an agreed signal (gentle nudge or a short knock on the table) to indicate that s/he will now read alone.

3. The child proceeds to read alone. If s/he meets a difficult word, the parent supplies the word. The child repeats the word, and both parent and child continue to read aloud together until the child feels comfortable enough to repeat the signal, indicating s/he is ready to read alone once more.

4.   Praise and encouragement are very important throughout this procedure.

5.   The parent or adult should discuss the story with the child — the events so far, the characters, predicting what might happen next.

6.   Paired reading can be seen as a transitional stage between reading together and reading alone. The child is supported in his/her reading and is reading for enjoyment and meaning. S/He is therefore not frustrated by difficulties with decoding unknown words.

(Topping, 1987)

Shared reading involves the parent reading to the child (Moloney, 2000). The enjoyment of books and exposure to many different types of books are of fundamental importance in developing a readiness to read. In class, the teacher and a group of children may use Big Books. Guided by the teacher, the children will read the pages together. This may be followed by word activities. The teacher may use the shared reading sessions to develop the children's phonological awareness. S/He may direct the children's attention to: recognising rhyming words; dividing words into syllables; counting the number of syllables in a word; thinking of words beginning with a given initial sound.

Note: The procedures mentioned above are based on the methods outlined in *Road to Reading: Your Child and You; A Practical Guide for Parents* and accompanying training video produced by the Curriculum Development Unit, Mary Immaculate College, Limerick.

DEVELOPMENTAL STAGES OF READING

If they are to be sensitive to the progress which children have already made in reading ("where child has come from"), teachers must be aware of the developmental stages of reading. They must also be aware of the next step ("where the child is heading") in reading development, from emergent literacy stage to becoming an independent reader.

Many researchers have outlined the development of reading skills. According to Frith (1985), the *Three Stages in the Development of Reading Skills* are:

1.   Logographic Stage

2.   Alphabetic Stage

3.   Orthographic Stage

The *Logographic Stage* involves:

▸▸   Recognition of whole words

▸▸   Building sight vocabulary

▸▸   Look-and-Say strategies used

Total immersion in a print-rich environment helps the child recognise the written words s/he already knows in spoken language. The shape of the word and the visual appearance of the letters of the word help the child in visually recalling the word.

The *Alphabetic Stage* means that the child can apply the "alphabetic principle" to words.

▸▸   Recognition of letter and sound correspondences

▸▸   Phonic skills for decoding

The child begins to recognise letter-name-sound correspondence. His/Her phonic knowledge is important as s/he develops word attack skills or strategies to decode new words.

The *Orthographic Stage* involves:

▸▸   Automatic recognition of words

▸▸   Using contextual cues to make sense of what is read

(Frith, 1985)

These three stages in the development of reading provide just one framework or explanation of the child's development in reading. There are other models in the literature.

At the first stage in this particular model, the Logographic Stage, the child is looking at the shape of the words and is using visual memory for word recognition.

The development of spoken language occurs in parallel with the recognition of whole words. The emphasis in the *English Language Teacher Guidelines* (1999) is on the development of good oral language skills as a prerequisite for the beginning reader.

At Stage 2, the Alphabetic Stage, phonic skills begin to develop. In recent years, there has been a trend toward introducing explicit *phonological awareness training* to children at the early stages in learning to read. It has been found that poor phonological awareness among children is an early predictor of dyslexic-type difficulties which may develop later. (See Indicators of Difficulties, page 77)

The learning objectives of phonological awareness training involve the improvement of syllabic awareness, rhyming awareness and phonemic awareness or awareness of individual sounds. Activities included as part of this training include practice in segmenting some or all of the sounds represented by the letters in a printed word.

Example

Isolating the beginning sound, the middle sound, the end sound

p a n — r a n   b i g — b o g   p e t — p e c k

Phonological processing and phonemic awareness are important at this development stage.

At Stage 3, the Orthographic Stage, the child has an automatic recognition of words and a wider reading vocabulary. S/He uses context clues to make sense of what s/he reads. The child has moved from "learning to read" to "reading to learn" and is on the way to becoming an independent reader.

In *Learning to Read: The Great Debate*, Chall (cited by Ott, see References), outlined the essential principles for the successful teaching of reading:

1.   Developing word recognition skills
2.   Using meaningful reading texts
3.   Building a sight vocabulary of whole words
4.   Teaching explicit phonics
5.   Using text-integrated phonics
6.   Providing controlled vocabulary

7.   Establishing reading readiness

8.   Teaching pupils according to reading ability levels

As all teachers are teachers of reading, these general principles apply to all reading instruction. It is no coincidence that the Learning Support Teacher is often known as the "Reading teacher". Children who are underachieving in literacy skills or who have specific learning difficulties of a dyslexic type may be referred to the Reading/LS teacher or to the Resource teacher for supplementary teaching.

TEACHING READING TO CHILDREN WHO ARE RECEIVING LEARNING SUPPORT

The *Learning Support Guidelines* (DES, 2000) recommend that the LST develop an "Individual Profile and Learning Programme" (IPLP) for each child who is receiving learning support. This programme will set out:

▶▶ Learning strengths and attainments

▶▶ Priority learning needs

▶▶ Learning targets

▶▶ Learning support activities to be undertaken by LST

▶▶ Learning support activities to be undertaken by the class teacher

▶▶ Learning support activities to be undertaken at home

(*Learning Support Guidelines*, p. 71)

(See also section on IEPs, page 51, for further information)

Taking each child's needs into account, supplementary lessons aimed at developing literacy skills should be planned for each individual child. (See section on "Diagnostic Assessment and Developing the Individual Education Plan", page 42)

SUPPLEMENTARY TEACHING IN READING AS RECOMMENDED BY LEARNING SUPPORT GUIDELINES

The principles which guided the *Reading Recovery Programme* devised by Marie Clay in New Zealand (1993) have influenced the rationale of Ireland's *Learning Support Guidelines*. These guidelines emphasise the importance of teaching children *strategies* which they can *use*.

In *Reading Recovery*, teachers look carefully at how children are reading, including the strengths they have and the miscues (errors) they make. The aim is to develop independent readers. A 30-40 minute session is recommended, with each session broken down into distinct parts.

▶▶   Practise what the child already knows until s/he is fluent (familiar reading).

▶▶   Revise and consolidate learning strategies (eg blending sounds, identifying new words).

▶▶   Set new tasks which allow existing knowledge to be used (give help in organising activity).

▶▶   Introduce new material — help child to think, problem solve, make predictions, use prior knowledge.

▶▶   Encourage self-correction.

One drawback seen in all teaching approaches to reading is that the children who are receiving learning support may become over-dependent on help from the LST, instead of becoming actively involved in their own learning.

The approach recommended in the *Learning Support Guidelines*, and supported by this author, is one that encourages independent readers who are active in their own learning.

As mentioned already, good readers will use a variety of strategies to read. The following section outlines those skills which are considered necessary to becoming a good reader.

NECESSARY SKILLS AND STRATEGIES

As the earlier discussion indicated, a necessary ability for learning to read is the ability to recognise that the words we hear are composed of individual sounds within the word. This skill is called *phonological awareness*. Specific instruction in phonological awareness has a positive effect on reading achievement.

The child receiving learning support will need training in the phonological skills s/he needs to develop. S/He needs to learn how to count the sounds in words, to segment the sounds and syllables in words and to recognise rhyming words. Children should learn the letters of the alphabet as well as the letter names and their sounds.

TEACHING PHONOLOGICAL AND PHONEMIC AWARENESS

▶▶ Break up sentences into separate words.

▶▶ Break words into syllables.

▶▶ Count syllables.

▶▶ Make up rhymes.

▶▶ Listen to nursery rhymes and rhymed stories.

▶▶ Use onset and rime activities to develop analogy for word families (s-and, h-and, st-and). Segment words into onset and rime.

▶▶ Segment words into phonemes.

▶▶ These activities will prepare the child for phonics and applying the alphabetic principle.

Examples of language activities which help build phonological awareness

▶▶ **Clapping names** — Ask children to clap out syllables in names and words. For example: clap Jen-ni-fer (3 claps) or e-lec-tri-ci-ty (5 claps).

▶▶ **Take away a sound** — Children say their names or a word without the initial sound. For example: say "-enjamin"; "-atasha"; "-ark".

▶▶ **Add a sound** — Say a pair of words, the second adding a sound: "girl, girls"; "mile, smile".

▶▶ **Deleting sounds** — Begin with removing syllables. For example: *playground*, say it without *play; steamboat*, say it without *steam*.

▶▶ **Auditory perception** — Say *coat*. Say it again without "c". Say *ball*, now say it without "b". Say *picnic*, say it again without *pic*.

▶▶ **Awareness of rhyming sounds** — Child listens to series of three words such as *ball, sit, wall* ; *hit, pie, tie* and tells which two words rhyme.

(Lerner, 2000)

WORD IDENTIFICATION — DECODING STRATEGIES

▶▶ Teach blending of letter sounds already known.

▶▶ Find the root word, prefixes and suffixes.

▶▶ Examine common word endings.

▶▶ Divide words into syllables, using two- and three-syllable words.

▶▶ *Basic sight vocabulary* should be relevant and meaningful to the child.

COMPREHENSION STRATEGIES — USING CONTEXT CLUES

▶▶ Encourage child to reflect on the text: discuss it, write about it.

▶▶ Use dictionaries.

▶▶ Find word meanings from context — Use *cloze procedures*.

▶▶ Sequence ideas in the text.

▶▶ Use comprehension strategies such as survey, question, read, recall, review (SQ3R).

▶▶ Set predicting assignments.

PREDICTING, CHECKING, USING COMPREHENSION STRATEGIES

▶▶ Get child to confirm and check what s/he has read.

▶▶ Ask questions: "What do you think this story is going to be about? What word would make sense here?"

▶▶ Use cloze procedures to help child predict.

▶▶ Teach child to scan the text and look at the layout of the chapter.

▶▶ Skim the material to get an overview of what it is all about.

Reading teachers are often confused about the terminology surrounding the skills necessary to manipulate sound segments in words.

▶▶ *Phonemic Awareness* — awareness of individual sounds in words

a-t   m-a-n   f-r-o-g

▶▶ *Phonological Awareness* — awareness that language is composed of different sounds

car-pet   m-an

▶▶ *Phonics* — teaching of letter/sound correspondence

Phonemic awareness involves an understanding of the sounds in the *spoken language.* For example, the child can tell you that "bat" is made up of three sounds: b-a-t. S/He knows that if I take the "t" from "cart", I will have "car". This ability is highly predictive of success in learning to read, particularly in learning to decode.

Phonological awareness is an understanding of the larger units of sound such as syllables, onsets and rimes. Activities and games such as recognising rhymes and alliteration, breaking words into syllables and counting syllables when hearing them in a spoken word will help to develop the child's phonological awareness.

Phonics is the explicit teaching of the alphabetic principle of letter/sound relationships.

Good practice suggests that there should be a reciprocal relationship between phonics and oral language. Interaction with print, combined with explicit attention to the sound structure in spoken words, is the best way to approach early instruction in reading which necessitates combining phonemic awareness, oral language development and a print-rich environment.

REFERENCES

Clay, M. (1993). *Reading Recovery: A Guidebook for Teachers in Training.* New Zealand: Heinemann.

Department of Education & Science (2000). *Learning Support Guidelines.* Dublin: The Stationery Office.

Department of Education & Science, National Reading Initiative (2001). *The English Curriculum (Primary): Approaches to the Teaching of Reading …a guide to the video.* Dublin: The Stationery Office.

Frith, U. (1985). "Beneath the surface of developmental dyslexia". In K.E. Patterson, J.C. Marshall & M. Coltheart (Eds). *Surface Dyslexia: Neuropsychological and Cognitive Analysis of Phonological Reading.* London: LEA.

Government of Ireland (1999). *Primary School Curriculum: English Language Curriculum.* Dublin: The Stationery Office.

Lerner, J. (2000). *Learning Disabilities, Theories, Diagnosis and Teaching Strategies.* Boston: Houghton Mifflin Company.

Moloney, N. (2000). *Road to Reading: Your Child and You — A Practical Guide for Parents.* Limerick: Curriculum Development Unit, Mary Immaculate College, Limerick.

Phonemic Awareness. Position Statement of the Board of Directors of the International Reading Assocation (1999).

Ott, P. (1999). *How to Detect and Manage Dyslexia.* Oxford: Heinemann.

Reason, R., & Boote, R. (1994). *Helping children with Reading and Spelling.* London: Routledge.

Topping, K. (1987). "Paired Reading: A Powerful Technique for Parent Use", *The Reading Teacher* 40 (7), 608-614.

Westwood, P. (1993). *Commonsense Methods for Children with Special Needs.* London: Routledge.

USEFUL LISTS AND CHARTS

THE MAIN COMPONENTS OF EARLY PHONOLOGICAL AWARENESS PROGRAMME

▸▸   Listening games and activities

▸▸   Listening to and reciting nursery rhymes

▸▸   Rhyming pairs

▸▸   Odd-one-out Phonological Awareness rhyming cards

▸▸   First-sound pairs

▸▸   Odd-one-out first letter cards

ORDER OF INTRODUCING LETTER SOUNDS — 1

Continuant consonants	f, l, m, n, r, s, v, z
Stop consonants	b, c, d, g, h, j, k, p, qu, t, w, y, x
Vowels in initial position	a, e, i, o, u
CVC onset + rime	m–an, c–ot, r–un

INTRODUCING LETTER SOUNDS — 2

Initial consonant blends — onset + VC rime						
▸▸ bl-	cl-	fl-	gl-	pl-	sl-	
▸▸ br-	cr-	dr-	fr-	gr-	pr-	tr-
▸▸ tw-	sc-	sp-	st-	sw-		
▸▸ scr-	spl-	tr-	etc.			

INTRODUCING LETTER SOUNDS — 3

Consonant digraphs + VC rime	ch– sh– wh– th–
Vowel + final consonant blend rimes	n–est b–end s–and
Onset + vowel digraph rime	b–ean h–air
Introduce as they arise in reading material	

EXTENDING PHONOLOGICAL AWARENESS

Vowel + long vowel rimes	c–are t–ake m–ore f–ine
Phonemic analysis	What 2 sounds are in "at" "if" "on" "up"? (3 / 4 sounds?)
Structural analysis	adding –ed, –s, –er, –ing, ("paint")
Introduce simple syllabication	car`pet, ro`bot

ONSET AND RIME — INTERMEDIATE STAGE BETWEEN PHONEME AND SYLLABLE

Word	Onset	Rime
At		–at
Him	h–	–im
Shop	sh–	–op
Stand	st–	–and
Strand	str–	–and
Say	s–	–ay

(*Phonological Awareness*, A copy of handout distributed to teachers during Revised English Curriculum In-service, Department of Education and Science, October 2001)

THE HIGHEST FREQUENCY WORDS WHEN LEARNING TO READ

The following 12 words make up an average of one-quarter of all words in reading.

a	and	he	I	in	is	it	of
that	the	to	was				

The following 20 words, when added to those above, make up one-third of all words in reading.

all	as	at	be	but	are	for	had
have	him	his	not	on	one	said	so
they	we	with	you				

When the following 68 words are added, they constitute the 100 words which make up one-half of all reading.

about	an	back	been	before	big	by	call
came	can	come	could	did	do	down	First
from	get	go	has	her	here	if	Into
just	like	little	look	make	made	more	me
much	must	my	no	new	now	off	old
only	or	our	other	out	over	right	see
she	some	their	them	then	there	this	Two
up	want	well	went	were	what	when	where
which	who	will	your				

Note: These words should never be taught as a list. They should be used, whenever possible, in meaningful contexts. They can be used in reading games or dictation and when writing. The list may also be used in specific cases for diagnostic purposes.

(© Philomena Ott, 1999

Handout distributed at International Reading Conference, Dublin, 2000)

Essential Reading Vocabulary*

from *Reading as Communication: An Interactive Approach* by FB May

anything	give	great	Mrs.	says	very
and	at	when	about	time	than
a	could	group	night	should	want
because	do	have	nothing	some	water
in	be	can	out	has	first
again	does	head	of	something	was
is	this	use	then	look	called
almost	done	knew	brother	the	were
another	door	heard	on	sometimes	wanted
that	or	an	them	more	oil
always	buy	know	off	their	what
it	had	each	these	write	its
any	enough	light	one	they	where
are	four	only	long	who	thought
he	by	which	so	go	now
been	from	dog	other	there	father
for	but	she	her	see	down
both	friend	many	own	through	goes
brought	full	might	people	to	work
as	words	how	make	number	day
house	don't	money	put	together	you
with	not	if	like	no	did
city	live	mother	right	today	would
some	gone	Mr.	said	two	your
his	all	will	him	way	get
year	they're	school	our	there's	once
I	we	up	into	my	find
made	may	part			

Teaching Goal: To have the children recognise these words through visual memory within one second, preferably at the end of first class and not later than second.

Good testing procedures require that these words be arranged randomly rather than in alphabetical order.

To test, have the child start with the *anything* column and read the 7 words. Then move on to the next column (*give*) and so on.

220 WORD BASIC SIGHT VOCABULARY

Preprimer	Primer	First	Second	Third
1. the	45. when	89. many	133. know	177. don't
2. of	46. who	90. before	134. while	178. does
3. and	47. will	91. must	135. last	179. got
4. to	48. more	92. through	136. might	180. united
5. a	49. no	93. back	137. us	181. left
6. in	50. if	94. years	138. great	182. number
7. that	51. out	95. where	139. old	183. course
8. is	52. so	96. much	140. year	184. war
9. was	53. said	97. your	141. off	185. until
10. he	54. what	98. may	142. come	186. always
11. for	55. up	99. well	143. since	187. away
12. it	56. its	100. down	144. against	188. something
13. with	57. about	101. should	145. go	189. fact
14. as	58. into	102. because	146. came	190. through
15. his	59. than	103. each	147. right	191. water
16. on	60. them	104. just	148. used	192. less
17. be	61. can	105. those	149. take	193. public
18. at	62. only	106. people	150. three	194. put
19. by	63. other	107. Mr.	151. states	195. thing
20. I	64. new	108. how	152. himself	196. almost
21. this	65. some	109. too	153. few	197. hand
22. had	66. could	110. little	154. house	198. enough
23. not	67. time	111. state	155. use	199. far
24. are	68. these	112. good	156. during	200. took
25. but	69. two	113. very	157. without	201. head
26. from	70. may	114. make	158. again	202. yet
27. or	71. then	115. would	159. place	203. government
28. have	72. do	116. still	160. (American)	204. system
29. an	73. first	117. own	161. around	205. better
30. they	74. any	118. see	162. however	206. set
31. which	75. my	119. men	163. home	207. told
32. one	76. now	120. work	164. small	208. nothing
33. you	77. such	121. long	165. found	209. night
34. were	78. like	122. get	166. Mrs.	210. end
35. her	79. our	123. here	167. thought	211. why
36. all	80. over	124. between	168. went	212. called
37. she	81. man	125. both	169. say	213. didn't
38. there	82. me	126. life	170. part	214. eyes
39. would	83. even	127. being	171. once	215. find
40. their	84. most	128. under	172. general	216. going
41. we	85. made	129. never	173. high	217. look
42. him	86. after	130. day	174. upon	218. asked
43. been	87. also	131. same	175. school	219. later
44. has	88. did	132. another	176. every	220. knew

Source: D.D. Johnson, "The Dolch List Re-examined", *The Reading Teacher*. 24, 455 — 456, 1971. (The 220 most frequent words in the Kucer-Francis corpus)

SIGHT WORDS I CAN READ (1)

Basic Words 1 — 10				
the	of	and	am	to
in	is	you	that	it

Basic Words 11 — 20				
he	was	for	on	are
as	with	his	they	at

BONUS Naming Words				
girl	boy	house	sun	school
tree	door	dog	cat	toy

Basic Words 21 — 30				
be	this	have	from	or
yes	no	had	by	we

Basic Words 31 — 40				
but	not	what	all	were
was	can	your	when	said

Basic Words 41 — 50				
there	use	an	each	which
she	do	how	their	if

BONUS Naming Words				
apple	lunch	mother	father	man
clown	box	rain	bike	grass

Basic Words 51 — 60				
will	up	other	about	out
them	then	so	her	would

Basic Words 61 — 70				
less	these	some	those	more
funny	little	many	happy	long

Basic Words 71 — 80				
make	like	him	into	time
has	look	write	go	see

SIGHT WORD LISTS © LADYBIRD/PENGUIN PUBLISHING

SIGHT WORDS I CAN READ (2)

Basic Words 81 — 90	who my	way than	been now	people keep	could call
Basic Words 91 — 100	find come	did may	day made	down part	get over
Basic Words 101 — 110	new me	take live	sound know	only place	work year
Basic Words 111 — 120	our just	give after	very good	thing name	most back
BONUS Naming Words	one six	two seven	three eight	four nine	five ten
Basic Words 121 — 130	think help	say much	great line	sentence through	where before
Basic Words 131 — 140	too tell	old want	mean came	right follow	same small
Basic Words 141 — 150	also form	show put	soon end	around another	set does
BONUS Naming Words	pet baby	sign kitten	book puppy	woman animal	game fish
Basic Words 151 — 160	well big	must turn	large here	because ask	even why

SIGHT WORDS I CAN READ (3)

Basic Words 161 — 170					
went	men	need	knew	land	
us	try	home	move	kind	

BONUS Action Words					
read	turn	laugh	ride	talk	
ate	jump	going	draw	hide	

Basic Words 171 — 180					
word	off	again	change	play	
spell	away	point	answer	air	

Basic Words 181 — 190					
still	world	study	should	learn	
high	near	every	own	found	

Basic Words 191 — 200					
first	next	last	below	love	
start	stop	light	thought	under	

Basic Words 201 — 210					
left	while	maybe	along	might	
close	few	open	something	seem	

Basic Words 211 — 220					
never	hard	always	together	begin	
life	those	got	group	often	

BONUS Naming Words					
body	hand	eye	head	face	
feet	earth	plant	city	food	

Basic Words 221 — 230					
both	until	between	important	side	
night	walk	sentence	please	sea	

Basic Words 231 — 240					
took	began	miss	carry	state	
once	hear	without	late	second	

SIGHT WORDS I CAN READ (4)

BONUS **Naming Words**	paper water	car story	money family	country children	road picture
Basic Words **241 — 250**	idea real	eat let	far above	enough sometimes	watch cut
Basic Words 251 **— 260**	soon pay	list leave	almost music	young round	song buy
Basic Words 261 **— 270**	being area	tiny mine	half friend	question problem	stand sure
BONUS **Action Words**	wish cry	sang save	heard found	wonder remember	listen notice
Basic Words 271 **— 280**	since order	ever today	piece better	usually best	easy whole
Basic Words 281 **— 290**	short fast	hour hold	early toward	reach passed	cover step
Basic Words 291 **— 300**	true colour	false circle	alike number	different underline	add mark
BONUS **Colour Words**	black white	green red	yellow orange	purple pink	brown blue

Note to Teachers or Parents: These lists contain the 300+ most frequently encountered words in the English language. An independent reader should be able to recognise them instantly on sight. These lists can be used for practice or to test children's word recognition skills.

PART 5

SPELLING

EFFECTIVE TEACHING STRATEGIES FOR SPELLING

The author wishes to acknowledge the ideas expressed in Brendan Culligan's *Improving Children's Spelling* which influenced some of the suggestions in this chapter.

WHAT MAKES A GOOD SPELLER?

SPELLING STRATEGIES USED BY GOOD SPELLERS

The following strategies contribute to effective spelling, even for those who are not "natural" spellers. Good spellers can generally be identified by the following:

▶▶ Familiar with common "letter strings".

▶▶ Pay attention to the internal structure of words, ie the root word, prefixes, suffixes.

▶▶ Understand serial probability of letters, ie understand that certain letters cannot follow others.

▶▶ Recognise common letter sequences or "chunks".

▶▶ Recognise that a word does not contain only consonants.

▶▶ Understand that most words contain at least one vowel.

▶▶ Realise that each syllable must contain a vowel.

▶▶ Use background knowledge, existing vocabulary and wide verbal ability to associate and make analogies.

▶▶ Learn and remember words as part of their reading experience.

▶▶ Remember spelling rules.

▶▶ Have good phonological knowledge — they can pick out the sounds in a word, then relate letter(s) to that sound when they need to write it.

SPELLING IS ESSENTIALLY A VISUAL SKILL

Spelling is essentially a *visual skill*. Visual recall is required to encode the word. While spelling is a writing activity, it develops more slowly than reading. While reading involves *decoding* words, spelling involves *encoding* words. The visual appearance of the word and the flow of letters provide important clues to the speller.

Teachers should concentrate on developing the child's visual memory in order to improve the *visual image* of the word. Children should be trained to look for visual patterns in words so they can "visualise" the word. While spelling is essentially a visual still, children do rely on their existing knowledge of sounds in words. This knowledge is helpful since the sounds of words in the English language are generally more regular than irregular.

REASONS FOR POOR SPELLING

There are many and varied reasons why children find spelling difficult.

With an over-emphasis on reading instruction and reading for meaning — and much less emphasis on writing and word study — many children have not had sufficient practice in developing good spelling strategies.

Some teachers believe that spelling is "caught", not "taught". For those children who seem to absorb everyday words quite naturally, this may appear to be the case.

For the child who is dyslexic or low-achieving, some of the following may be reasons for poor spelling ability.

1. **OVER-RELIANCE ON PHONICS AND SOUNDS**

    The child's phonic knowledge leads him/her to write irregular words as if they were regular. Although phonetically correct, the child has relied entirely on sound and therefore writes the word incorrectly.

    becos = because   sed = said   thay = they

    Over-reliance on phonics and sounds may be related to poor visual recall insofar as the child is depending totally on one learning approach, the auditory channel, to the exclusion of any visual image of the word.

2. **POOR VISUAL RECALL**

    A poor visual imagery for letter sequences means that the child does not have a mental picture of the whole word. The child relies on letter-by-letter copying, so when "correcting" misspellings, s/he may copy one letter at a time from each word and fail to retain a visual image of the complete word.

3. **POOR READING ABILITY**

    Good spelling does not develop in isolation. If a child has poor reading skills, s/he may also lack the phonic skills and decoding abilities which are helpful for effective spelling.

4.   INDIVIDUAL LEARNING STYLE

Individual children have preferences and strengths when it comes to imaging or perceptual recall. For some children, the preferred style of learning is the *visual channel*. In other words, visual learners need to *see* things in order to understand them fully. Pictures, shapes, colours, patterns — all help to embed their learning of new concepts.

Other children prefer the *auditory channel*. Auditory learners like to hear information. Listening to sounds, repetition of sounds and spoken words bring meaning to new concepts. This style of learning is the most usual form of classroom communication. However, not all children are auditory learners. Teachers must be aware of differing learning styles and teach to these differing styles — visual, auditory, tactile, kinaesthetic.

Some children need to touch and feel the texture, pattern and shape of letters and words to get a mental picture of the word. They are *tactile learners*. Sandpaper, plastic or magnetic letters are useful. A tactile approach succeeds with some learners.

Kinaesthetic learners need to move. Movement may involve tracing letters on the page or in the air, tracing in sand etc. Evidence suggests that encouraging "joined up" or "cursive" writing from an early age fosters a motor memory for letter strings, encouraging the development of efficient spelling. Movement of fine motor muscles when practising joined handwriting while simultaneously learning "letter strings" helps to internalise the new information.

5.   LONG-TERM MEMORY DIFFICULTIES

Just as adults write for meaning, children also need to associate writing with conveying meaning, or purpose. Parents often express frustration when spellings are learned at home by rote for homework, then are completely forgotten for Friday's test. The child knows the words at home — this is *instant recall* . But these words are not yet in the child's long-term memory and cannot be retrieved for his/her test. More importantly, s/he cannot transfer the learning to written work. The child may spend time spelling each word orally for an adult but this is not efficient learning. S/He needs to write each word and to see the associations or patterns in each word. This will help the child create a mental picture of the word so that s/he can retrieve it from his/her long-term memory at a later stage.

Children should begin with spelling words on a *personal need-to-know* basis. Only those words which are familiar and relevant should be learned. Make sure the words are already in his/her speaking and listening vocabulary and devise *personal dictionaries* — "Words I Need". Teach the child how to make analogies with other words with similar letter strings or letter patterns. This reduces the memory load and helps the child see the patterns in words.

Examples

<u>cle</u>ver — bicy<u>cle</u>   bro<u>ugh</u>t — ca<u>ught</u>   beca<u>use</u> — ho<u>use</u>

Subject words and special vocabularies may be included later on as they progress. Ask child to point out the troublesome part of the word; this is the only part of the word s/he needs to learn. Help him/her make an association… or find a visual link or pattern to transfer or to "cue" the difficult part of the word from a state of instant recall into his/her long-term memory. It is only when the information is meaningful in some way — ie obvious or witty or funny — that it will be easily recalled from long-term memory.

Mnemonics, picture clues and nonsense rhymes all help.

Encourage children to create their own clues to spelling — this will probably be more effective than the teacher's imagination!

6.   SELF-ESTEEM/MOTIVATION

The way in which a child perceives his/her spelling ability will affect his/her expectations about spelling. Just as in reading, encouragement and enjoyment come from a feeling of success, of being in control of the words. If a child has a poor self-image about spelling, s/he may respond by writing at random. Such a child cannot write "to order" and sees no purpose in written tasks.

The purpose of written expression is to communicate meaning. For the child with learning difficulties, spelling should not be seen as an "all or nothing" task but an effort to communicate meaning, with praise for approximate spellings. While every child may not be a good speller, every child can be a better speller.

STAGES OF SPELLING DEVELOPMENT

Children progress through a series of stages when learning to spell. Although the stages may sometimes merge into each other, a child has to progress through each one. Awareness of these stages gives an insight into providing the most effective support to the child in his/her writing. Understanding these stages will also help the LST to be realistic in his/her expectations of a child's spelling proficiency. If the LST is aware of the child's stage of development in spelling, s/he can aim to take the child to the next stage of development by teaching systematic and appropriate spelling strategies. These stages of spelling development as first outlined by Gentry (1981) are further discussed in Culligan (1997), Chapter 2.

▶▶ **PRE-COMMUNICATIVE STAGE**

At this early stage, the scribble looks like the child is writing intentionally. The scribbles may include drawing.

▶▶ **PRE-PHONETIC STAGE**

Child has some knowledge of letter formation, rudimentary shapes, names of letters. This may include a drawing, capital letters, and there may be an absence of vowels.

▶▶ **PHONETIC STAGE**

At this important stage, the child uses "invented", plausible spelling and shows some awareness of the sound structure in words (*phonological awareness*). Long vowel sounds are the most difficult, but the child begins to write/spell a word according to the way it sounds.

It is at this stage that a spelling strategy programme must be provided. When phonological knowledge is secure, children are ready to proceed to a *kinaesthetic visual strategy* or to a *multi-sensory strategy*.

▶▶ **TRANSITIONAL STAGE**

Although the different stages in spelling development often overlap, this transitional stage may take a long time for some children to reach. The child moves from reliance on sound to a visual awareness of the word, a sense of "does the word look right?".

Teacher intervention is important at this stage. Spelling proficiency will not happen automatically. The child must be shown that certain letter strings in words occur together.

Examples

ea in h*ea*d, s*ea*t and w*ea*ther

ich is in M*ich*ael, in R*ich*ard, and in M*ich*elle, despite different sound.

The child must learn to look closely at the structure of words, to be shown little words in bigger words. Letter patterns must be generalised and word families studied. In this way, the child gradually acquires a visual knowledge of words and the serial probability of letter sequences.

▸▸ **CORRECT/COMPETENT STAGE**

At this stage, there is a growing mastery of phoneme/grapheme relationships, a knowledge of basic spelling rules, and an awareness of word structures and irregularities.

Notes

▸▸ The LST encounters many children at the Phonetic Stage of spelling development.

▸▸ For the child with a learning difficulty or dyslexic-type difficulty, spelling should not become an "all or nothing" activity. Approximate spelling should be accepted. Avoid red biros ticking all incorrect words!

▸▸ Remember: joined handwriting clearly improves spelling.

▸▸ Ensure children are aware of the purpose of written work. If it is a piece of functional writing — for example, a dictation exercise — correct spelling will be expected, whereas creative work, such as story writing, will have greater emphasis on meaning and content.

DIAGNOSTIC ASSESSMENT OF SPELLING

STANDARDISED SPELLING TESTS

While standardised spelling tests — eg Schonell Graded Spelling Test, Daniels & Diack Spelling Test — give teachers a *spelling age* for the child, they do not tell them anything about the child's spelling ability.

The teacher needs a *diagnostic assessment* of the child's strengths and needs if s/he is to plan a positive intervention which teaches effective spelling strategies. The LST needs further information on the child's efforts at spelling in order to plan appropriately. S/He needs to find out more about the particular strategy a child is using in spelling and the way in which this strategy works for that child in his/her writing.

Peters (1970) mentions three attributes which aid in the prediction of spelling competence:

▶▶ Evidence of interest in words and an understanding of their use in a written form

▶▶ Visual perception of word form

▶▶ Carefulness and speed of handwriting

However, errors in spelling may present as visual errors, as auditory errors, as a result of poor letter formation (handwriting), or a combination of all three.

EXAMPLES OF VISUAL ERRORS

▶▶ Visual perception errors such as Reversals — b/d

▶▶ Visual perception errors such as inversions — u/n   m/w

▶▶ Visual sequential memory errors such as Transpositions — friend/freind   felt/ left

▶▶ Uses mixture of capitals and lower case

▶▶ Writes beginning letters only

▶▶ Spells phonetically — cannot revisualise — anser/answer   dun/done

EXAMPLES OF AUDITORY ERRORS

▶▶ Auditory discrimination errors — d/t   v/f   ch/sh   k/g

▶▶ Vowel sound confusion — pet = pat

▶▶ Omits vowels — brd = bird

▶▶ Omits final blend — rut = rust

▶▶ Uses synonyms — house = home

▶▶ Omits word endings — ed, s, ing

▶▶ Auditory sequential memory errors — aminal, hopsital

As part of a diagnostic approach, the Learning Support Teacher should look at the *type* of errors the child makes most frequently, not necessarily the *number* of errors. (Further explanation of these points is given on page 117, "Reasons for poor spelling")

HOW TO FIND OUT MORE ABOUT A CHILD'S SPELLING STRATEGY

▶▶ Look at the child's current written work. Look at several pieces of free writing/independent writing.

▶▶ Look at what the child *can do*.

▶▶ Use the *Stages in Learning to Spell* (below) in making decisions appropriate to the child's stage of development.

▶▶ Decide on the most pressing need for this child. It is not practical to concentrate on every spelling mistake.

▶▶ Refer to the chart to check child's stage of spelling mastery (refer also to the stages of spelling development mentioned above).

LEARNING TO SPELL: THE STAGES

STAGES IN LEARNING TO SPELL

The LST may find the following "Stages in Learning to Spell", as outlined by Reason and Boote (*1994,* p. 133), a useful guide in observing what the child can or cannot do. The purpose of diagnostic assessment of spelling is to establish the child's strengths and needs, and to set priorities.

Stage 1

▶▶ Recognises rhymes and rhyming words.

▶▶ Blends spoken sounds into words.

▶▶ Makes some representations of phonic structures in writing the beginnings of words.

Stage 2

Can write

▶▶ single letter sounds

▶▶ words such as: at, in, hat, sun, lid, net, dog (Consonant-Vowel-Consonant words — CVCs)

▶▶ some common harder words — have   went   likes

Can analyse words into constituent sounds — re-mem-ber; ch-ur-ch

Stage 3

Can write words with

▶▶ consonant digraphs — ch, sh, th

▶▶ consonant blends — sl-, fr-, sk-, -st, -nd etc.

▶▶ vowel digraphs — ea, au, ow

▶▶ magic "e" (came, mine etc.)

Spells most common words.

Stage 4

▶▶ Spells most words accurately.

▶▶ Knows when to use a dictionary.

SETTING PRIORITIES IN SPELLING

Instruction in spelling should be in the context of reading *and* writing… as part of a *Whole Language Approach*. The teacher sets priorities for spelling mastery based on the child's strengths and needs.

The first priorities must be to help the child:

▶▶ Use analogy in spelling — child becomes familiar with "onsets and rimes". The *onset* is the part of the syllable which precedes the vowel; the *rime* is the remainder of the syllable.

Examples

Word: shop Onset = sh- Rime = –op

Word: say   Onset = s- Rime = –ay

Word: cake Onset = c- Rime = -ake

▶▶ Identify syllables and segment words into syllables, first aurally, then visually. It is helpful to clap out the sounds, eg *te-le-phone, yes-ter-day*.

▶▶ Identify regular words which conform to spelling patterns — teach the *spelling rule* backed up by visual materials, games, dictation etc.

Example

Rule: Before adding a suffix to a CVC word, double the final consonant.

run (root word) runner, running

wet (root word) wetter, wettest

big (root word) bigger, biggest

Example

Rule: There is always an "e" after "v" at the end of words in English — have, save, love.

▶▶ Become familiar with and consolidate short vowel sounds.

TEACHING STRATEGIES: STRUCTURED APPROACHES TO TEACHING SPELLING

Children should be presented with a *structured approach* to learning spelling. Otherwise, they may not benefit from seeing the patterns and structure in written language.

Samples of teaching approaches include:

▶▶   Look, Cover, Write, Check

▶▶   Simultaneous Oral Spelling

▶▶   Fernald Method

▶▶   Cued Spelling

LOOK, COVER, WRITE, CHECK

Margaret Peters (1985) emphasised the importance of visual skills in learning to spell. Verbal ability, visual perception of word form and perceptuo-motor ability all influence spelling ability. Charles Cripps (1978) also supported a visual strategy for learning new words.

The *Look, Cover, Write, Check* method is an effective and clearly defined classroom strategy for learning new words which individual children want to know how to spell.

▶▶   *Look* — Look at the internal structure of the word. Associate it with other known words. Look for words within words.

▶▶   *Cover* — Cover up the word to be written. If the child needs to look again, let them look, but they should cover the whole word again before writing more letters.

▶▶   *Write* — Try it out.

▶▶   *Check* — Compare with the original. Try again if it's wrong.

This strategy is self-regulating — many children enjoy the challenge of getting it right.

A variation of this method is *Look, Say/Trace, Cover, Write, Check*.

Some children may need to say or trace the word before writing it. If so, the teacher introduces this stage before the child covers the word. Child may need to say the word in syllables, or small parts.

At the Look/Say/Trace stage, encourage the child to visualise the word by "taking a photo of it" in his/her head! The child may need to look at it again, so guide him/her to look at the tricky bits. Teacher should demonstrate the complete process of *Look, Cover, Write, Check* so the child becomes aware of how s/he learns best.

SIMULTANEOUS ORAL SPELLING (SOS)

This is a multi-sensory method suited to teaching children who are dyslexic. For children who do not automatically relate the sounds to the visual images of print, this will help them to categorise sounds and improve their phonological awareness. This approach to teaching spelling has been adapted by Bradley (cited in Reid, 1999, p. 112). The procedure is as follows:

▶▶ Child chooses word to be learned.

▶▶ Have the word written correctly, or made with the letters.

▶▶ Child reads the word.

▶▶ Child writes the word in cursive script, *saying the letter names as s/he writes*.

▶▶ Child checks attempt to see if it is correct.

▶▶ Continue to practise the word in this way over a period of six days.

▶▶ Child is led to generalise from this to other words which sound and look alike.

> *Combining SOS with cursive writing is the most effective strategy of all.*
>
> (Montgomery, 1990)

FERNALD METHOD

This is another multi-sensory approach which works well with children who have good visual skills. It is also used to teach reading and spelling. Lerner (1997) outlines the following steps:

Child is told s/he is going to learn words in a new way which has proved very successful.

▶▶ Child selects a word s/he wishes to learn.

▶▶ Step 1. Word is written by the teacher. Teacher says the word.

▶▶ Step 2. Child traces the word, saying it several times, then writes it on piece of paper while saying it.

▶▶ Step 3. Child writes the word from memory without looking at original copy.

▶▶ If word is incorrect, child repeats step 2.

▶▶ If word is correct, the word is put in a file box. These words are used later in stories.

▶▶ Child uses the word in a sentence or a story.

"CUED SPELLING"

This spelling technique makes use of *paired reading* and *peer tutoring* techniques.

The child works with a helper (another child or adult) who assists with his/her efforts to remember the "cues" to spelling a word correctly. As in paired reading, praise and encouragement are important at every stage.

There are ten steps in this approach.

1.	Speller chooses word.

▼

2.	Check the correct spelling of the word, then write it down.

▼

3	Read the word... helper and speller together and speller alone.

▼

4.	Choose cues — eg a "long vowel sound"; "it sounds like…"; "there are two beats in this word"; "there's a silent letter at the end" etc. Speller notes the "tricky" parts of the word and chooses the "clues" to remember them eg: friend = Fri (day) end could = our flame = long "a" sound

▼

5.	Say the cues together.

▼

6.	Speller says cues and the helper writes the word.

▼

7.	Helper says cues, speller writes the word.

▼

8.	Speller says cues (unaided) and writes the word.

▼

9.	Speller writes the word as quickly as possible.

▼

10.	Speller reads the word.

Remember — the helper praises the speller at each stage!

Each day, review all the "cues" and "clues" as outlined in the steps again. The speller writes all the words quickly and checks. If the words are wrong, repeat above ten steps.

(Topping, as cited in Reid, 1998, p. 125)

GOALS OF A CLASS SPELLING PROGRAMME

While no single approach holds the key to successful spelling, the following ideas for classroom teaching of spelling will provide teachers with practical and effective strategies. The Revised Curriculum advocates a multi-dimensional approach to the teaching of spelling.

WHOLE LANGUAGE APPROACH

While the teacher may concentrate on improving a child's reading ability, the importance of an integrated programme of reading, oral language and spelling cannot be over-emphasised. Oral language development is an integral part of this approach. Creative writing, spelling and handwriting are not separate activities. Children should not be expected to spell words which they do not understand and which are not in their receptive vocabulary.

CHILDREN WHO FIND SPELLING DIFFICULT NEED:

▶▶ Words which follow basic phonic and spelling pattern (70% words)

▶▶ Most frequently used words

▶▶ Words which child will need in his/her next piece of writing

▶▶ Individualised lists

▶▶ Topic words

▶▶ Work on specific words misspelled in free writing sessions, eg "Words to Remember" or "Words to Watch"

▶▶ A range of games and word puzzles for reinforcement

▶▶ Joined writing (also called cursive script)

▶▶ Individual progress charts

▶▶ Lists of words for regular review and assessment

▶▶ Daily attention to spellings; Weekly revision; Testing for mastery

SPECIFIC TEACHING STRATEGIES

▶▶ If a child can write one syllable at a time, teach him/her to use this strategy by building on the auditory channel, the *Sound Symbol* approach. Develop an effective strategy for each child — eg syllable break-up, onset and rime, or Look/Cover/Write/Check technique.

▶▶ Link phonics with spelling basic regular words, as in onset and rime and syllable division. (The *Phonological Awareness Training Programme* is a good resource.)

▶▶ Teach similarities in words, regardless of sound — eg h*ome*, w*ome*n; M*ich*ael, R*ich*ard, wh*ich*.

▶▶ Use personal alphabetic word book/personal dictionary to help children take responsibility for their own spelling.

▶▶ Remember — creative writing, spelling and handwriting are not completely separate activities.

▶▶ Children will need irregular words as soon as they begin to write — *people, brought, they*. Use a basic spelling vocabulary such as: *Basic Spelling Vocabulary* (Reason & Boote, 1994) and *Core Words* (Culligan, 1997).

▶▶ Give the child practice in using the target words in context by writing sentences or stories or by sending a message to someone — eg use bulletin board in classroom, children leave messages for each other, teacher leaves message for child.

▶▶ Dictation practice may be a half-way house between writing a word in isolation and in the context of a story. Regular dictation helps long-term memory.

▶▶ Teach cursive writing and practise writing letter strings — this fosters *motor memory* of letter sequences.

IDEAS FOR TEACHING SPELLING IN THE CLASSROOM

▶▶ *Pre-test/Post-test Strategy* — Child keeps list of words needed — "Words I Find Difficult", "Words I Need" — and attempts to spell these words by writing them with the aid of a strategy. Afterwards, the child looks carefully at "difficult parts" of the word and examines any errors. Help child to develop his/her own "clues" and visual memory associations for the difficult part of the word.

▶▶ *Sight Words* (high-frequency words) — Children dictate the words to each other. Teacher may spot-check the progress or mark the tests.

▶▶ *Snap game* — instant recognition of sight words… two of each word card.

▶▶ *Dictation exercises* — Teacher can check the learned spellings or "approximate" spellings. Recommended resources: dictation sentences in *Spelling in Context* (Peters and Smith 1993 p. 69); and in *Improving Children's Spelling* (Brendan Culligan 1997 p. 91).

▶▶ Use *closure exercises* to check for learned vocabulary — eg *hospital* "The nurse looked after the patient in the __ __ __ pital."

▶▶ *Closure exercises* can also be used where child chooses possible letter combinations for a given word:

> enough
>
> __ __ ough
>
> en __ __ gh
>
> enou __ __
>
>
> does
>
> do __ __
>
> __ __ es

▶▶ *Hangman* — Child uses plastic alphabet; letters and vowels are indicated in different colours.

▶▶ *Shannon's Game* — First letter is given but second letter must be chosen before moving onto third etc. (*serial probability*). Alert children to possible patterns; to possible choices that don't fit.

▶▶ *Newspaper Detective* Game — Sunday paper magazines are useful for games: finding prefixes, suffixes. Use highlighter pens (check for target spellings first).

▶▶ *Alphabetical Order* activities.

▶▶ *Dictionary skills* — Divide dictionary into sections to help with quick location of an initial letter — eg towards beginning for D, towards end for T and in the middle for M.

▶▶ Spelling by *syllables* — Syllable sounds.

▶▶ *First names, Surnames* — How many smaller words can I make from my name?

▶▶ Use *Word Searches* for reinforcement only. Word searches do not replace teaching a spelling strategy (letters in word search should preferably run from left to right and top to bottom; for weaker pupils, words going only left to right).

▶▶ *Anagrams* — lean/lane stop/post teach/cheat (not for weak spellers).

▶▶ *Words in words* — Look closely… bra in the li*bra*ry! tree in the *street*… spit in ho*spit*al; lice in po*lice*… eyes = e + *yes*.

▶▶ Memorable ways of remembering irregular words constantly misspelled need to be discovered — eg friend = *I fried my friend on Friday*

▶▶ *Mnemonics* memory aids — Can You Cook Large Eggs? = cycle. Encourage children to create their own "clues" — humorous and visual, use pictures.

▶▶ *Word Families*

our — colour, courage, favourite, flour

ear — pear, learn, heart, wear

eve — clever, eleven, never, seven

▶▶ Use colour for different syllables — change colour:

can di date   man u fac ture   pen cil

▶▶ *Visual supports in the classroom* in the form of charts.

▶▶ Models of the Look, Cover, Write, Check process.

▶▶ Lists of words which look the same.

▶▶ Word banks set up according to letter strings.

▶▶ Supply of Look-and-Say words on teacher's desk — Children refer to these but do not take the word card from the desk. In this way, they are encouraged to visualise the word and revisit it if unsure.

CLASS CHART FOR SPELLINGS

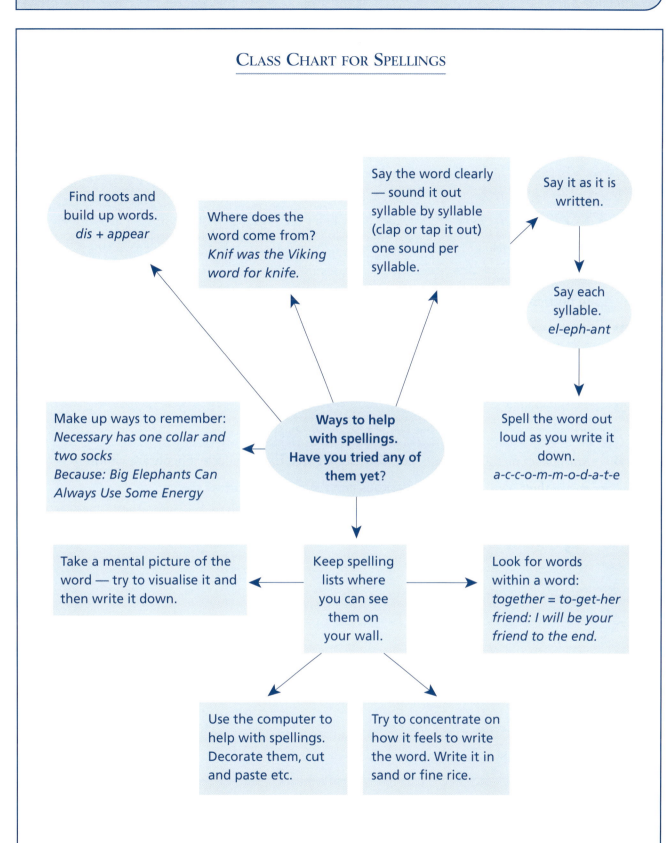

Find roots and build up words.
dis + appear

Where does the word come from? *Knif was the Viking word for knife.*

Say the word clearly — sound it out syllable by syllable (clap or tap it out) one sound per syllable.

Say it as it is written.

Say each syllable. *el-eph-ant*

Make up ways to remember: *Necessary has one collar and two socks* *Because: Big Elephants Can Always Use Some Energy*

Ways to help with spellings. Have you tried any of them yet?

Spell the word out loud as you write it down. *a-c-c-o-m-m-o-d-a-t-e*

Take a mental picture of the word — try to visualise it and then write it down.

Keep spelling lists where you can see them on your wall.

Look for words within a word: *together = to-get-her* *friend: I will be your friend to the end.*

Use the computer to help with spellings. Decorate them, cut and paste etc.

Try to concentrate on how it feels to write the word. Write it in sand or fine rice.

REFERENCES

Bradley, L., & Bryant, P. (1985). *Children's Reading Problems*. Oxford: Blackwell Press.

Cripps, C. (1978). *Catchwords: Ideas for Teaching Spelling*. London: Harcourt, Brace & Jovanovich.

Cripps, C. (1991). *A Hand for Spelling Book 1, 2, 3*. Cambridge: Learning Development Aids.

Culligan, B. (1997). *Improving Children's Spelling: A Guide for Teachers and Parents*. Dublin. Elo Press.

Fernald, G.M. (1943). *Remedial Techniques in Basic School Subjects*. New York: McGraw Hill.

Gentry, J.R. (1981). "Learning to spell developmentally". In *The Reading Teacher* 34.

Lerner, J. (1997). Learning Disabilities: Theories, Diagnosis and Teaching Strategies. Boston: Houghton Mifflin.

Montgomery, D. (1990). *Children with Learning Difficulties*. London: Cassell Educational.

Peters, M. (1985). *Spelling: Caught or Taught?* London: Routledge.

Peters, M. L., & Smith, B. (1993). *Spelling in Context: Strategies for Teachers and Learners*. Windsor: NFER-Nelson.

Reason, R. & Boote R. (1994). *Helping children with reading and spelling. A special needs manual*. London: Routledge.

Reid, G. (1998). *Dyslexia: A Practitioner's Handbook*. England: John Wiley & Sons.

Tod, J. (2000). *Individual Education Plans: Dyslexia*. London: David Fulton Publishers.

Topping, K.J. (1995). *Paired Reading, Spelling and Writing*. London: Cassell.

Topping, K.J. (2001). Peer and Parent Assisted Learning. In Reading Association of Ireland *Reading Matters: A Fresh Start*. Ireland.

Westwood, P. (1993). *Commonsense Methods for Children with Special Needs*. London: Routledge.

USEFUL TEXTS

Brand, V. (1989). *Spelling Made Easy — Multi-sensory Structured Spelling*. Royston: Egon Publishers.

Hope, D. (2001). *The Complete Phonic Handbook*. New Ross: RIC Publications/ Prim-Ed Publishing.

Hornsby, B. & Shear, F. (1980). *Alpha to Omega — The A-Z of teaching reading, writing and spelling*. London: Heinemann.

Reason, R., & Boote, R. (1994). *Helping Children with Reading and Spelling. A special needs manual*. London: Routledge.

Shiel, G., & Murphy, R. (2000). *Drumcondra English Profiles*. Dublin: Educational Research Centre.

Wilson, J. (1993). *Phonological Awareness Training: A New Approach to Phonics*, (PAT Programme). University College London: Educational Psychologists Publishing.

PART 6

MATHEMATICS

THE MATHEMATICS CURRICULUM

WHY LEARN MATHS?

"Mathematics encompasses a body of knowledge, skills and procedures that can be used in a rich variety of ways: to describe, illustrate and interpret; to predict and to explain patterns and relationships in *Number, Algebra, Shape and Space, Measures and Data.* Maths helps to convey and clarify meaning…

Mathematics education should seek, therefore, to enable the child to think and communicate quantitatively and spatially, solve problems, recognise situations where mathematics can be applied and use appropriate technology."

(Department of Education & Science, *Mathematics*, 1999, p. 2)

Maths is an essential tool for both child and adult. Some children, however, will have difficulty in acquiring competence in basic math skills. As with all academic subjects, success in mathematics depends on successful, positive learning experiences. Many adults today say they hated maths at school and are still "no good at maths". They may admit that they could never do maths and perceived it as "hard". As a result of these experiences, certain career choices may have been closed to them.

When encountering maths, frequent problems faced by many students include difficulties in:

▶▶ Basic computation skills

▶▶ Problem-solving skills

▶▶ Mathematical language problems

Basic computation will present difficulties for a large number of children who already have learning difficulties, especially since abstract symbols are used to record the basic operations of addition, subtraction, multiplication and division. A child who may be operating at a concrete level of understanding may also be unable to abstract beyond this level without support.

Problem-solving may also be difficult for this child. S/He may not be able to carry out the correct maths operation, or may not know which operation to use.

Understanding mathematical terms may be an added problem as the language of mathematics is precise and accurate.

WHY CHILDREN EXPERIENCE LEARNING DIFFICULTIES

The *SERC Report* (1993, p. 76) described pupils in need of remedial teaching as follows: "…those pupils in ordinary first level and second level schools who have clearly observable difficulties in acquiring basic skills in literacy and/or numeracy or who have some difficulties of a more general nature."

It is important to remember that pupils with difficulties are individuals with many of the same needs as other pupils. Along with these *common* needs, they may also have *exceptional* needs arising from characteristics shared by some others, eg dyslexia, speech and language disability. In addition, some children will also have *individual* needs which are different from all others.

This section will address the needs of the following groups of children:

▶▶   The child who is under-achieving/who learns slowly

▶▶   The child with speech and language disability

▶▶   The child with poor attention span/attention difficulty

▶▶   The child with specific learning disability (SLD)/dyslexia

Generally speaking, these children need the teacher to notice first their learning difficulty, and then to adjust or adapt the lesson and the teaching materials. Differentiated instruction has long been practised by effective class teachers to meet the individual needs of children with learning difficulties.

THE CHILD WHO IS UNDER-ACHIEVING

Maths is a sequential subject which builds upon concepts and skills already learned. If a child has a shaky foundation in maths, s/he may not be able to relate new concepts and skills to what s/he already knows.

For the child whose maths progress is significantly below expectations for his/her age and class level, the teacher must teach basic number skills. This child may have gaps in sequential learning and is at risk of falling further behind the rest of the class. Abstract symbols may have been introduced too early without any concrete materials or real-life examples. Concrete materials play a very big part in helping the child to see *what* is happening and understand *why* it is happening, as with subtraction.

TEACHING POINTS

▶▶ Provide materials at *concrete level* to represent number facts — unifix cubes, Dienes blocks, coins, squares. Then proceed to *representational (semi-concrete) level* — tallies, pictures, bundles, scorecards — before moving on to *abstract symbols*— %, fraction, decimal.

▶▶ Use less verbal elaboration in lesson: *peer tutoring* and *cross-age tutoring* can work well. Children in both helper and learner roles will benefit equally.

▶▶ Concentrate on teaching number facts and number relationships — eg 78 is "nearly" 80; 107 is a "bit more than" 100.

▶▶ Link new math concepts and skills to existing knowledge. "What do we already know about percentages? What does this sign mean — '25% off TV and video'?"

The less able child will frequently make errors in basic facts and will need opportunities to review and check his/her work.

Games are powerful motivators. Card games, magic squares, dominoes etc. provide opportunities for reinforcing basic number facts in an enjoyable way. Less able pupils will need more time to understand visually the representation of number facts before moving on to the abstract level of representation by symbols.

Practical activities in maths, demonstrations by the teacher and physical experience with the materials will provide opportunities for understanding the concepts. Although some children will take longer to acquire basic math skills than their peers, they will make steady progress with the proper support.

THE CHILD WITH SPECIFIC SPEECH AND LANGUAGE DISABILITY

This child will have difficulty with mathematical language and the terms used in developing mathematical concepts.

LANGUAGE IN MATHEMATICS

The *Primary School Curriculum Teachers' Handbook* (Department of Education,1971, p. 128) states:

"Language is the basis of conceptual thought and as such has a fundamental importance in the learning of mathematics. Although mathematics is chiefly concerned with the study of relationships and their expression in symbolic form, it should be remembered that words come before symbols to the child. By putting his thoughts into words, he comes to grasp the relationships more easily and later, the symbols become more understandable to him. It is generally recognised that concept formation in children is accelerated when the *appropriate language is associated with experience*. The teacher should therefore supply the necessary mathematical vocabulary to enable the child to express his ideas more accurately."

Language in maths is a major source of difficulty to many children. To those with specific language disability, it is an extra disadvantage.

There are many variations in the words commonly used to signify addition, subtraction, multiplication, division, equals. Teachers themselves often use different words to signify specific mathematical activities: eg minus… subtract… decrease… less than… take away. Such language can be confusing to the child when used in different contexts.

Mathematical language is necessarily precise. For the child with a specific speech and language disability, comprehension of words used during math lessons may be weak. For example, "take away" may signify a Chinese meal or a sum. The "second division" may represent a football league or a part of long division sum.

The *Revised Curriculum* emphasises the need for guided discussion and group interaction during maths activities. Discussion skills at every level and in each of the strands of the curriculum are given added importance in the revised programme. Delaying the introduction of symbols until the children are familiar with the precise language required will be of great benefit to those children with language comprehension difficulties.

A child's use of language will give the teacher an insight into his/her strengths and needs in the subject. Encouraging the child to give answers orally and to explain how s/he solved the problem will deepen understanding of maths concepts.

TEACHING POINT

New terms to be introduced in maths should be taught thoroughly and not left to incidental learning.

THE CHILD WITH POOR ATTENTION SPAN/ATTENTION DIFFICULTY

The child with an attention deficit is characterised by attention skills which are developmentally delayed or inappropriate, accompanied sometimes by impulsivity. If the condition also involves hyperactivity, it is referred to as Attention Deficit Hyperactivity Disorder (ADHD).

Characteristics of children with Attention Deficit Disorder (ADD) can include the following:

▶▶ Difficulty in remaining seated

▶▶ Fidgeting with hands or feet

▶▶ Difficulty following through on instructions

▶▶ Shifting from one uncompleted task to another

▶▶ Difficulty in playing quietly

▶▶ Interrupting conversations and intruding on other children's games

▶▶ Appearing not to listen to what is being said

▶▶ Doing things that are dangerous without thinking about the consequences

(DES, 1999)

TEACHING POINTS

Suggested teacher interventions during maths lesson which may prove helpful include:

▶▶ Position the child's desk near the teacher. This will allow for regular reminders to stay on task and to give praise for work attempted so far.

▶▶ Keep desk clear of clutter to minimise fidgeting.

▶▶ Praise and reward as much as possible for sitting still and listening.

▶▶ Keep directions short and simple and clear.

▶▶ Ensure the maths task is at an appropriate level.

▶▶ Keep the task short.

▶▶ Change the activity regularly. This will help concentration.

▶▶ Colour coding and highlighting worksheets/blackboard work may help.

THE CHILD WITH SPECIFIC LEARNING DISABILITY (SLD)/DYSLEXIA

The difficulties experienced by children with Specific Learning Disability may result from several different factors.

Not all children with an SLD will have difficulties in mathematics. However those children who have difficulties in sequencing, short-term memory, language comprehension or spatial perceptual problems will present with problems when it comes to understanding mathematical concepts.

Potential difficulties which may affect these children's performance in mathematics include:

▶▶ Difficulty with the language of mathematics

▶▶ Sequencing difficulties

▶▶ Directional confusion

▶▶ Short-term memory difficulties

▶▶ Anxiety/stress

▶▶ Organisational/spatial problems in maths

DIFFICULTY WITH THE LANGUAGE OF MATHEMATICS

The child's comprehension of language and symbols may be weak. For example, the child may not understand that +6 also means "plus 6", "add 6", "increase by 6". If the child's reading skills are weak, s/he will take longer to read accurately and may miss an important part of the mathematical story problem. Mathematical terms may be confused: for example, *calculate* may be read as *classify*; the word *diagram* may be read as *diameter*; *value* may be read as *volume* (Henderson, 2000).

There are many different words which mean *subtract — minus, less, decrease, take away*. The child needs to read with accuracy and speed or s/he will miss the sense of the question.

SEQUENCING DIFFICULTIES

A child may have difficulty counting, especially counting beyond 10 or 20. Counting backwards may be especially difficult, even with the help of the number line to visualise the sequence of numbers in both directions. S/He may find it hard to see the *pattern* in numbers such as odd and even numbers, or counting in twos, in fives, in tens.

At a later stage, the child may not remember the sequence of steps to follow for long multiplication, long division etc.

DIRECTIONAL CONFUSION

Just as letters may be reversed by the child with a dyslexic-type difficulty, so too numbers may be reversed or the order reversed — 6 and 9; 17 becomes 71.

The starting point for addition may cause problems. In maths, the child must start at the right (with units) and work left with tens and then hundreds. After spending a long time getting used to reading and writing from left to right, we now tell the child to start an addition sum at the *right* and move *left*!

This may cause a problem for some children. Further difficulties arise when the direction of division appears inconsistent, as in these examples.

$$\frac{14}{3} \qquad 14 \div 3 \qquad 3\overline{)14}$$

SHORT-TERM MEMORY DIFFICULTIES

Recalling basic number facts may be difficult for some children. A poor short-term memory can create problems in working out mental arithmetic tasks. When a child is unable to "hold" information in his/her short-term memory while working out a basic number fact, his/her working memory becomes overloaded. S/He may not have automatic recall of basic number facts (tables, basic number bonds) and so must work it out each time it is required. This extra overload will cause the child to lose sight of the overall sum.

Example

From a group of 60 children, 28 travel to school by car. The rest travel by bus. How many travel by bus?

The child with short-term memory difficulties may concentrate on subtracting 8 from 0, then remember to "borrow 1" and "pay back 1" — and may forget the overall sum in the process. The teacher can help by showing the child strategies which will lessen the load on short term memory.

28 is 2 less than 30   30 is half of 60   30 + 2 is the answer

ANXIETY/STRESS

Fear, stress and poor self-image all contribute to a child's anxiety about his/her mathematical ability. Such a child may avoid maths entirely rather than attempting a question which s/he may get wrong. As mathematics builds on what the child already knows, no new learning will take place under such feelings of stress. The child will not take a risk for fear of getting it wrong.

The child with a learning difficulty will take longer to work out a problem because of poor knowledge of basic facts. S/He will be slower at writing and may lose his/her place when copying. Presentation and organisation of work will be more haphazard.

The child may feel "I'm no good at maths so I'll fail" and this can become a self-fulfilling prophecy. Maths lessons can become a huge source of stress, and the greatest difficulty seems to be the anxiety attached to the subject.

ORGANISATIONAL/SPATIAL PROBLEMS IN MATHEMATICS

A child with learning difficulties may have problems copying work from the blackboard and may skip or repeat numbers when copying. The plus sign (+) may be copied as x (multiply). S/He may have difficulty relating two-dimensional diagrams to three-dimensional objects and shapes. In the early stages of numeracy development, children in general may have problems with place value. But for children with learning difficulties, problems with place value may persist beyond the early numeracy stage. Questions such as "What is the value of 6 in the following numbers — 246; 1624; 60?" can cause great difficulty. Further difficulties may arise with position of the decimal point.

PRIORITY AREAS FOR CHILDREN WITH LEARNING DIFFICULTIES IN MATHS

▸▸ BASIC number skills — strategies to teach

▸▸ Problem-solving skills — suggested approaches

▸▸ Mathematical language

The *Revised Curriculum in Maths* has introduced some changes in content and methodology which will particularly benefit the child with a difficulty in this subject.

▸▸ Estimation skills

▸▸ Mathematical language

▸▸ Discussion skills in maths

▸▸ Problem-solving skills

▸▸ Practical activities, constructivist approach (delay using symbols to record as long as possible)

NUMBER

Difficulties with number will be easily observed. The child may have difficulty with basic number facts due to poor short-term memory.

Research has shown that teaching children different thinking strategies facilitates their learning and the retention of the basic facts; they also learn to transfer these strategies to other problems. Some children will develop these strategies spontaneously but others will need explicit teaching.

TEACHING POINTS

Commutative law of addition and multiplication

7 + 3 is easier to learn than 3 + 7 (count on from larger number)

7 x 9 = 9 x 7 nine sevens is one seven less than ten sevens (70) 70 - 7 = 63

Two facts (addition and multiplication) can be learned for the price of one!

Addition strategies

▸▸ Addition of zero to number doesn't change the number.

9 + 0 = 9   37 = 0 + 37

▶▶ Teach "doubles" 4 + 4   7 + 7   9 + 9

▶▶ Teach "near doubles" (one less than double)   4 + 3   7 + 6   9 + 8

▶▶ Teach plus 10 — observe effect on number relationships.

▶▶ Use number square.

▶▶ Teach number bonds to 10 (all the number facts that make up 10)

▶▶ Use discovery methods with child — help child to see patterns.

▶▶ Show subtraction as another side of number bond — If child knows and sees
6 + 4 = 10, then 10 - 6 = 4

▶▶ Help child to count on "one more"/+ 1

▶▶ Help child to count on "two more"/+ 2 until this becomes an automatic strategy for
him/her to use.

Multiplication

▶▶ Teach "doubles"   7 × 7   6 × 6   5 × 5

▶▶ Teach "near doubles"   7 × 6   6 × 5   5 × 4

▶▶ Teach effect of multiplication by 1 on basic multiplication facts
eg 1 × 8 = 8   8 × 1 = 8
Number to be multiplied remains the same — demonstrate with objects.

▶▶ Teach multiplication by 10. This is a key number, as the 10x table facts can be extended
to work out 5× and 9× tables.

▶▶ Pattern in 5× table — digit ends in 0 or 5

▶▶ 9× table is one less than 10.
(see also pattern in number — all facts in this table add up to 9!)

▶▶ Teach child to see where number fits into the number system and its relationship to
other numbers. "Is 72 a large number? Is it closer to 100 or closer to 20?"

As numeracy is so basic to mathematics, the child with difficulty in this area may never be exposed to the various other aspects of mathematics. It is therefore important that his/her experiences in maths are not limited because of difficulties in the number area.

The child may enjoy the creative side of maths; this will boost his/her self image at maths. Activities involving shape and space will help him/her see maths in the environment. S/He can find shapes and angles in everyday life, and can use his/her reasoning powers to work out size of angles once s/he can recognise a right angle of 90°.

LEARNING SUPPORT IN MATHEMATICS

> *Effective supplementary teaching in mathematics involves diagnostic assessment, individual programme planning and instruction as well as record keeping.*
>
> (*DES*, 2000)

The same principles which apply to learning support in reading also apply to mathematics. The *Learning Support Guidelines* (DES, 2000) outline specific intervention in the area of mathematics.

STEP 1

Assessment of learning difficulties in mathematics

Formal assessment will be carried out by standardised testing which compares the child's progress in maths in relation to other children in the country.

The teacher may use *informal tests* such as checklists and teacher-made tests, gathering more information through discussion with other teachers and child's parents.

Children who are underachieving in maths as identified by their class teacher may be referred to the Learning Support Teacher for extra help.

STEP 2

Children who are identified as underachieving in mathematics or who have difficulties in this subject may be referred to LST for further testing. Consultation with class teacher and parents' consent are a necessary part of the process.

Diagnostic assessment by the LST will answer the following questions:

▶▶ What is the pupil's present level of (maths) knowledge?

▶▶ What gaps exist in his/her present maths understanding?

▶▶ What strategies does s/he use?

▶▶ What are the priority learning needs?

In order to prioritise and plan supplementary teaching, the LST must observe closely how the child approaches maths tasks and analyse the errors s/he makes. This process is similar to the one suggested for diagnostic testing in literacy.

The widely used standardised maths test may not pick up on the individual child's errors and the individual strategies the child uses. Each child brings a unique combination of strengths, learning style and individual needs and preferences to the learning situation. The LST will need to see the child working at a variety of mathematical tasks in order to pick up on his/her specific difficulties. The LST will also have to observe the child using concrete materials to determine his/her grasp of maths concepts. Discussing the topic and using maths language will guide the LST to identify gaps in present understanding. The teacher is then in a position to ascertain the learning style or *cognitive style* which the child uses to approach tasks.

COGNITIVE STYLE

Cognitive style refers to the way in which a person thinks through a problem. The literature supports the belief that children approach a mathematical problem with an individual learning style.

Bath (1986) investigated cognitive style in mathematical learning among children who are dyslexic. He identified the two extremes of a continuum and described these learning styles as "Inchworm" and "Grasshopper". The Inchworm will approach a maths task step-by-step, relying on a single method and using the numbers exactly as given. In contrast, the Grasshopper will look at the overall problem and is more likely to estimate, more inclined to break down and build up numbers, and will take a holistic view of the problem. There is no value judgment in either approach.

(Bath, Chinn & Knox, 1986)

A European-funded study, the Comenius Project 2000, looked at cognitive style used in solving mathematical problems among a group of pupils in specialist schools in England, the Netherlands and Ireland. The results in the three countries showed that children with dyslexia are more restricted than their non-dyslexic counterparts in their approach to problem-solving in mathematics. The majority of these children tended towards the "safe" and consistent method, the Inchworm approach.

Teachers need to be aware of the distinct learning style of a pupil in order to be more effective and teach to the child's learning style.

Flexibility in learning style can be encouraged, as the "Realistic Mathematics" (Freudenthal Institute) programme in the Netherlands has shown.

Ireland's *Revised Curriculum in Mathematics* places greater emphasis on "mental calculations, estimation and problem-solving skills", thus encouraging a more flexible learning style in maths.

RECORDING THE INFORMATION — DEVELOPING THE IEP/IPLP PROCESS

Supplementary teaching in mathematics must be planned and recorded for a specific period of time. Collaboration with the class teacher is necessary. An Individual Education Plan (IEP) or Individual Profile & Learning Programme (IPLP) may be used. (See section on Planning Individual Programmes, page 51.)

Useful diagnostic information may be obtained from the child's recent class tests, standardised tests and teacher-made revision tests. Having gathered information from all relevant sources, including parents, the LST will record all information onto an IEP or IPLP.

The LST must first take an in-depth view of what the child can do already in the area of math skills and the strategies s/he uses. The priority learning needs can then be determined, followed by the setting of specific learning targets. The LST may look at the "Strands" of mathematical abilities as outlined in the *Primary School Curriculum — Mathematics* (1999) to ascertain the gaps in the child's present knowledge, keeping in mind the level and progress of the main class.

REFERENCES

Bath, J.B., Chinn, S.J., & Knox, D. (1986). *Test of Cognitive Style in Mathematics*. New York: Slosson.

Chinn, S.J., & Ashcroft, J.R. (1993). *Mathematics for Dyslexics: A Teaching Handbook*. London: Whurr.

Chinn, S.J. (1997). *What to do when you can't learn the times tables*. Herts: Egon.

Chinn, S.J., McDonagh, D., Van Elswijk, R., Harmsen, H., Kay, J., McPhillips, T., Power, A., Skidmore, L. (2001). Classroom studies into cognitive style in mathematics for pupils with dyslexia in special education in the Netherlands, Ireland and the UK, British Journal of Special Education, 28, (2) pp. 80-85.

"Classroom studies into cognitive style in mathematics for pupils with dyslexia in special education in the Netherlands, Ireland and the UK", *British Journal of Special Education*, 28 (2).

Crookes, F. (1998). Helping with Dyslexia. Curriculum Advisory and Support Service, CASS, Southern Education and Library Board, Department of Education, Northern Ireland.

Curriculum Advisory and Support Service, Department of Education, Northern Ireland.

Department of Education (1971). *Primary School Curriculum: Teacher's Handbook Part 1* (1971). Dublin: Government Publications.

Department of Education & Science (2000). *Learning Support Guidelines*. Dublin: The Stationery Office.

Department of Education & Science (1999). *Primary School Curriculum – Mathematics: Teacher Guidelines*. Dublin: The Stationery Office.

Henderson, A. (2000, Oct.). "Maths and Dyslexia". Paper presented at Dyslexia Conference, UCD, Dublin.

Irish National Teachers Organisation (INTO). (date not recorded). *Learning Difficulties: Mathematics*, Volume 2. Dublin: Author.

Special Education Review Committee. *SERC Report* (1993). Dublin: The Stationery Office.

Westwood, P. (1993). *Commonsense Methods for Children with Special Needs*. London: Routledge.

PART 7

INFORMATION TECHNOLOGY IN THE CLASSROOM

ANN JACKSON
NATIONAL TECHNOLOGY AND SPECIAL NEEDS ADVISOR

- ICT and Special Needs Planning
- Children Needing Help with Writing Skills
- Ideas to Promote Writing Skills on Computer
- Using a Word Processor
- Technology and Special Education: Useful Contacts
- Using the Internet for Information & Resources
- Irish Web Addresses
- Websites for Educational Software

The author wishes to acknowledge Ann Jackson, National Technology and Special Needs Advisor, for contributing this section.

INFORMATION AND COMMUNICATION TECHNOLOGY & SPECIAL NEEDS PLANNING

Successful implementation of technology in education for students with special needs requires structured, informed, whole school and classroom planning. These are some of the general issues which could be considered.

SCHOOL PLANNING

SCHOOL CURRICULUM PLANNING

▶▶ There should be a collaborative and consultative process that involves all the school staff, with the support and cooperation of the Board of Management.

▶▶ There should be agreed aims and objectives for the use of technology as a learning support for children.

▶▶ Staff should research the current technology options available for the specific school population or individual students, as necessary. Be aware of low-tech options.

▶▶ There should be plans for regular in-service training of teachers and other staff in the use of standard and specialised technologies.

▶▶ It is important and beneficial to involve parents in the planning and training.

SCHOOL ORGANISATIONAL PLANNING

▶▶ Consider the provision and organisation of an appropriate range of ICT resources, including standard computer systems with standard and specialised software for both pupils and staff.

▶▶ Children will benefit from having access to computer resources on a regular basis.

▶▶ Pupils will need varying degrees of supervision and assistance.

▶▶ An ICT coordinator could oversee the planning and use of ICT equipment for SEN children.

▶▶ It is essential to plan the timetabling and rotation of ICT equipment, as necessary.

▶▶ Maintenance, repair and upgrading of ICT equipment must be considered.

▶▶ Funding of ICT equipment needs to be carefully researched and coordinated, including grants for equipment for individual pupils.

▶▶ Provision should be made for the safe storage and insurance of all school ICT equipment.

▶▶ There should be clear policy on Health and Safety issues and procedures for staff, students and visitors using ICT equipment. This should include guidelines on seating of pupils and positioning of equipment.

▶▶ There should be a supportive policy on staff training in ICT, both to support curricular implementation and administrative tasks.

▶▶ There should be a policy on the provision and use of e-mail and internet facilities for both pupils and staff.

CLASSROOM PLANNING

CLASSROOM CURRICULUM PLANNING

▶▶ ICT must support the individual educational needs of children.

▶▶ The teacher should decide which subjects and skills should be supported and which activities and tasks should be facilitated by ICT.

▶▶ ICT should be used to support teaching as well as learning.

▶▶ ICT can be used to produce materials for use away from the computer — for the classroom, for homework and even for leisure.

▶▶ There is an increasing range of suitable user-friendly software available for use with children with special needs. They should be carefully chosen and used to meet their needs.

▶▶ An outline of each child's use of ICT should be included in their Individual Education Plan or file.

▶▶ Consultation and collaboration with parents is essential, especially if the pupil is using ICT at home.

CLASSROOM ORGANISATIONAL PLANNING

▶▶ There should be easy access to the range of ICT equipment and devices needed by the group of children in the classroom.

▶▶ The ICT equipment should be positioned in the classroom, resource room or computer room so that it is easily accessible by staff and pupils, while still conforming with the school's Health and Safety Policy.

▶▶ The seating and positioning of each child using ICT should be evaluated and reviewed regularly.

▸▸ A height-adjustable trolley is a practical option which will enable different pupils to use equipment properly and safely, as well as allowing the system to be moved around as necessary.

▸▸ ICT systems should be positioned so that children are not isolated from the teacher and their peers.

▸▸ Computers must be placed so that glare from lights and windows is avoided.

▸▸ Space should be left around the computer so that collaborative work and social learning can be organised.

▸▸ Laminated instruction sheets, with procedures for using specific devices, connections and software displayed near the computer, can be useful for all staff and pupils.

▸▸ Software should be stored safely but should also be easily available as needed.

▸▸ ICT provides an invaluable resource for teachers and other staff for both information and communication. Staff should have access to both e-mail and internet within the school.

CHILDREN NEEDING HELP WITH WRITING SKILLS

The following children will benefit from help with their writing skills.

▸▸ Children with general learning difficulties

▸▸ Children who have language deficits

▸▸ A child who is a poor reader

▸▸ Child with specific learning difficulties

▸▸ Child who is reluctant to write

▸▸ Child who is under-achieving

▸▸ Child with hand-function deficits

▸▸ Child who is awkward or clumsy

▸▸ Child learning English as a second language

TECHNOLOGY

In general, these students:

▸▸ use the computer as an augmentative means of writing

▸▸ use standard input devices — keyboard and mouse

▸▸ use standard output devices — speech and printer

The exception to this will be students with physical disabilities, sensory impairments and significant hand-function deficits who may need to:

▸▸ use the computer as an alternative means of writing

▸▸ use specialised non-standard input devices

▸▸ use specialised non-standard output devices

SOFTWARE

Students may need to be able to use standard writing packages such as Word, Powerpoint, Publisher or other Desktop Publishing programs.

However, some students may need to use programs designed to give them extra support, along with resources such as speech output, easy-to-access graphics, word banks and whole word facilities.

Choice of software must be based on the needs, age and interests of the individual child.

IDEAS TO PROMOTE WRITING SKILLS ON COMPUTER

▶▶ Give child a title plus a short paragraph to stimulate ideas and get over the block of a blank page or no ideas.

▶▶ Use an interesting picture to stimulate ideas. Pictures can be from books, posters, art class etc. or on the computer — from a word processor (WP), clip-art or scanned into program.

▶▶ Use a series of very short sentences for child to expand. This can be used to expand vocabulary, practise spelling, or even as basis for a grammar lesson.

▶▶ Present a paragraph or two of concise text. Get the pupils to expand it while keeping the overall meaning. Then reverse the process.

▶▶ For the more reluctant child, enlarge text size. This means s/he has to write less to fill the page.

▶▶ Experiment with varying the font — find what suits the individual child.

▶▶ Get child to colour-code selected text — eg colour all nouns red, all verbs green etc.

▶▶ Instant grammar practice — An extension activity is to change all nouns or adjectives etc. to opposites or alternatives to make a funny story.

▶▶ Encourage children to aim for a perfect copy before printing.

▶▶ Teach children all the features of the WP package which s/he needs or is capable of using.

▶▶ Allow speech feedback if speech quality is acceptable and the child benefits from this. It can be supportive and even considered a reward.

▶▶ Teach children the difference between the formats for answering questions and writing essays. Short answers and incomplete sentences may be acceptable to show comprehension of text, for example, but an essay needs full sentences in a planned sequence, paragraphs and good layout.

▶▶ For slow writers/typers, essays might be "mapped" or "charted" first: eg title plus a word or phrase to outline each paragraph, then at least first paragraph fully written. Flow diagrams or linear plans might be used.

▶▶ Step-by-step organisation of written text:

Write down ideas.

Expand into sentences.

Punctuate.

Check spelling.

Proof read.

Save or print.

▶▶ For children who are particularly weak, try introducing several elements into the task — eg drawing, clip-art, word-art. Alternatively, allow child who makes a special effort a reward at end of session — game, computer art etc.

▶▶ Finally: "If the student doesn't learn the way we teach, can we teach him/her the way s/he learns?"

These are just some ideas for using the computer with children who need support with developing and consolidating writing skills. Remember: using the computer for writing is just substituting a blank screen and keyboard for a blank sheet of paper and a pen. Many students need some extra support or scaffolding.

USING A WORD PROCESSOR

Many students enjoy "writing" when they can do it on the computer. Typing can be a useful and necessary alternative to writing for many children with special needs.

ADVANTAGES

▶▶ Clear, legible *print-out* of finished text.

▶▶ *Mistakes* can be easily corrected.

▶▶ Text can be *moved*, *copied* and *amended* easily.

▶▶ Text can be *stored* for later completion.

▶▶ *Graphics* can be added.

▶▶ Often, text can be *spoken out*.

▶▶ *Spelling* can be checked and *dictionary* updated.

▶▶ *Font* size and type can be customised to suit the user.

▶▶ Often option to use a *thesaurus*.

▶▶ A *predictive* utility can be useful to some pupils.

▶▶ Pupils may dictate text using *voice recognition* software.

▶▶ *Preview* text before printing.

▶▶ Easy access to different *styles* and *formats*.

▶▶ Can use *word count* facility.

▶▶ *Editing*, *revision* and *correction* right up to print time.

▶▶ More *motivational* than pen and blank sheet of paper.

DISADVANTAGES

Child needs:

▶▶ Some basic *keyboard skills*.

▶▶ Some basic *mouse skills*.

▶▶ Spell-check facility is not a *magic answer*: eg need some word recognition skills.

▶▶ Basic *"writing" know-how*: eg some understanding of words, sentences, paragraphs, word order, spelling and punctuation.

▶▶ Reasonable range of *vocabulary*.

Teachers might find it useful to make up a checklist of pre-writing skills which would apply to children starting to "write" on the computer as well as using pen and paper. Skills would include letter recognition, upper case/lower case correlation, some spelling skills, basic understanding of words and sentences, basic grammar and syntax rules etc.

TECHNOLOGY AND SPECIAL EDUCATION

USEFUL CONTACTS

This is a basic list of software suppliers in Ireland and publishers of UK software, as well as some Irish contacts which might be useful for teachers working with students with special needs. It is not a definitive list but could be used as a starting point. Details given are those available at time of print. Teachers and others buying software for children with special needs are advised to get information from professional and impartial sources — other teachers, advisors etc. — before purchasing.

IRISH SUPPLIERS

Diskovery Educational Software
10 The Stables Office Park
Portmarnock, Co. Dublin
Tel: 01 803 8822
Fax: 01 803 8977
E-mail: info@diskovery.ie

Edtech Software Ltd
Murrisk
Westport, Co. Mayo
Tel: 098 64886
Fax : 098 64886
E-mail: edtech@oceanfree.net

Carrolls Educational Supplies
Unit 5, Western Industrial Estate
Naas Road
Dublin 12
Tel: 01 456 7280
Fax: 01 456 9998

Prim-Ed Publishing Ltd
Bosheen
New Ross
Co. Wexford
Tel: 051 440 075
Fax: 051 422 982

Demac Educational Software
36 Creighan Drive
Cavan
Tel/Fax: 049 433 2539

Andrews Award Systems Ltd
38 Pine Valley Park
Grange Road, Dublin 16
Tel: 01 493 0011
Fax: 01 494 4252
E-mail: awardsys@iol.ie

Jackson Technology

24 Kiltipper Ave., Aylesbury, D 24

Tel : 01 451 8508

E-mail : djackson@iol.ie

CodiCom

Corville, Roscea, Co. Tipperary

Tel: 0505 21198

E-mail : info@codi-com.com

UK SUPPLIERS

Inclusive Technology Ltd

Saddleworth Business Centre

Huddersfield Road

Delphi

Oldham OL3 5DF

Tel: +44 1457 819790

Fax: +44 1457 819799

Web: www.inclusive.co.uk

SEMERC

Granada Learning/SEMERC

Granada Television

Quay Street

Manchester M60 9EA

Tel: +44 161 827 2927

Fax: +44 161 827 2966

Web: www.semerc.com

Other useful sources include Sherston, Don Johnston, R.E.M., Crick Software, Tag Developments, SPA, Anglia, Fisher Marriott and Topologika. Check websites for contact details.

IRISH CONTACTS

NCTE

National Centre for Technology in Education

Dublin City University, Dublin 9

Tel: 01 700 8200   Fax: 01 700 8210   E-mail: info@ncte.ie

ScoilNet

Network for Irish Schools set up under auspices of NCTE

Web: www.scoilnet.ie

ICT Advisors

Based in most Education Centres. Information from Centres or NCTE.

Ann Jackson

National Technology & Special Needs Advisor based in CRC, Clontarf, D3.

Tel: 01 805 7545

E-mail: ajackson@crc.ie

Using the Internet for Information and Resources

INTERNATIONAL WEBSITES

European Agency
http://www.european-agency.org

Basic Skills Agency
http://www.basic-skills.co.uk

British Educational & Communications &
    Technology Agency — Becta
        http://www.becta.org.uk/technology/infosh
        eets/sen.html

Learning Disabilities Information &
    Resources
http://www.ldonline.org

Special Educational Resources on the
    Internet
http://www.hood.edu/seri/serihome.html

Teachers Evaluating Educational Multimedia
http://www.teem.org.uk

European Schoolnet
http://www.eun.org

ERIC Ed Resources Information Centre
http://www.eric.ed.gov.

Depart of Ed UK
http://www.dfes.gov.uk/sen

Computers in Ed Advisory Unit
http://www.advisory-unit.org.uk

MAPE — Micros in Primary Ed
http://www.mape.org.uk

Learning & Teaching Scotland
http://www.LTScotland.com

NASEN — National Association of Special
    Education Needs UK
http://www.nasen.org.uk

ASSISTIVE TECHNOLOGY

AbilityNet
http://www.abilitynet.co.uk

Center for Applied Special Technology —
    CAST
http://www.cast.org

Abledata, USA
http://www.abledata.com

Microsoft Accessibility Options
http://www.microsoft.com/enable/

SPECIALISED SUPPORT GROUPS & ORGANISATIONS

British Dyslexia Association
http://www.bda-dyslexia.org.uk

Dyslexia Association of Ireland
www.dyslexia.ie

Dyslexia Institute, UK
http://www.dyslexia-inst.org.uk

ICAN
http://www.ican.org.uk

Aphasia
http://www.afasic.org.uk

NASEN — National Association of Special
Education Needs UK
http://www.nasen.org.uk

Pavilion — section on ADHD & ADD
http://www.pavilion.co.uk

Autism UK
http://www.autism-uk.ed.ac.uk

RNIB — Royal National Institute for the
Blind
http://www.rnib.org.uk

RNID Royal National Institute for the Deaf
http://www.rnid.org.uk

SCOPE Disability Federation
http://www.scope.org.uk

Downs Syndrome Association
http://www.downs-syndrome.org.uk

Dyslexia International
http://www.dyslexia.com

ADHD Information Centre
http://www.adhd.co.uk

PIN — Parents Information Network UK
http://www.pin.org.uk

IRISH WEB ADDRESSES

ILSA — Irish Learning Support Association
http://www.ilsa.ie

IATSE — Irish Association of Teachers in
Special Education
http://www.iatseireland.com

NCTE — National Centre for Technology in
Education
http://www.ncte.ie

Scoilnet
http://www.scoilnet.ie

Department of Education
http://www.irlgov.ie/educ/

CRC — Central Remedial Clinic
http://www.crc.ie

Online Resources for Teachers
http://www.teachers.ie

Enable Ireland
http://www.enableireland.ie

INTO — Irish National Teachers
Organisation
http://www.into.ie

AHEAD (Higher Education Authority)
http://www.ahead.ie

Dyslexia Association of Ireland
http://www.dyslexia.ie

National Parents Council
http://www.edunet.ie

Websites for Educational Software

iAnsyst Ltd	http://www.dyslexia.com
Ablac Software	http://www.ablac.co.uk
Anglia Multimedia	http://www.anglia.co.uk
Crick Software	http://www.cricksoft.com
Don Johnston Special Needs Ltd	http://www.donjohnston.com
Granada Learning	http://www.granada-learning.com
Inclusive Technology	http://www.inclusive.co.ukk
Rickitt Education Media	http://www.r-e-m.co.uk
SEMERC	http://www.granada-learning.com
SPA	http://www.spa.org
Sherston	http://www.sherston.com
Widgit	http://www.widgit.com

GLOSSARY

ACID Arithmetic, Coding, Information and Digit span subtests of the Weschsler Intelligence Scale for Children, also known as the *ACID Profile*. These subtests give a profile of the child's strengths and weaknesses. Research has noted that poor scores in certain subtests may be linked with dyslexia.

ADD Attention Deficit Disorder. Characterised by attention skills that are developmentally delayed or inappropriate. Poor concentration and impulsivity also evident.

ADHD Attention Deficit Hyperactivity Disorder. Attention Deficit accompanied by hyperactivity; a neurological disorder.

Anomia Word-finding difficulties. This refers to the retrieval of stored words (the "tip of my tongue" feeling). Low-frequency words and multi-syllable words cause most difficulty. Children with dyslexia often find it difficult to retrieve "stored" information, or written words, from their long-term memory.

Automaticity Automatic recall of learned information. Fluency in reading requires automatic recall of certain basic words.

Big Books Books produced in a large format for collaborative reading with groups. Also known as "large format books".

Cloze procedure. Child must provide missing word as an aid to comprehension.

Cluster A group of letters which frequently occur together, for example -ear, -ing, -ant, -use.

Cue A clue to help predict the correct answer. Child may get clue from the context, from the semantics, from the sound of the word or letter pattern. This may be in reading or in spelling. For example cle occurs at end of bicycle.

Decoding A skill used in reading unknown words. The ability to break down difficult words.

Difficulty When learning does not happen easily, in spite of good teaching and adequate ability.

Disability Where a difficulty is so severe and persistent as to constitute severe difficulty in terms of learning.

Discrepancy A difference between abilities in separate areas, eg reading attainment and oral language ability; or reading comprehension and listening comprehension.

Disorder Refers to the constitutional (biological/neurological) origins of developmental delay.

Dyscalculia Severe difficulty with mathematical skills and concepts.

Dysgraphia Severe difficulty with written expression.

Dyslexia Defined as a Specific Learning Disability (SLD) affecting reading, spelling or writing.

Dysorthographia Severe difficulty with spelling.

Dyspraxia Severe difficulty in directing one's motor movements.

Educational Psychologist Psychologist with qualifications in education and psychology. Able to make an educational assessment of academic potential.

Expressive Language The two main components of oral language are receptive language and expressive language. Expressive language difficulties refer to problems producing appropriate spoken and written language.

Figure Ground A term to describe perceptual difficulties. Auditory figure ground: may be unable to attend to important auditory stimuli by pushing all other stimuli into background. *Visual figure ground*: may be unable to perceive a foreground figure against a background.

Grapheme The smallest unit of written language, ie a letter of the alphabet.

IQ Relates to the Intelligence Quotient as obtained on an intelligence test. It is calculated as follows:

$$IQ = \frac{MA \ (Mental \ Age)}{Chronological \ Age} \times 100$$

Information-carrying Units The phonemes in words or syllables in words which help the learner to decode.

Kinaesthetic Technique Teaching methods using body movement, gross motor and fine motor movements to assist learning.

LST Refers to the Learning Support Teacher. As outlined in the Learning Support Guidelines (2000): the primary work of the LST is the provision of supplementary teaching to pupils who experience low achievement and/or learning difficulties. (p.24)

Language Impaired (LI) Term used by speech pathologists in USA to describe speech and language disability, spoken language problems.

Letter String "Cluster" or "group" of letters which occur in a word, eg -ome occurs in some, come, home; -ing is in thing, nothing, bring.

Long-term Memory Permanent memory storage that retains information for an extended period of time.

Memory The mental activity of remembering, retaining and recalling information.

Miscue As in errors in reading. *Miscue Analysis* means assessment of frequent errors in reading in order to plan effective remediation. Similarly in spelling, analysis of errors made provides information to teacher about the learner's difficulties.

Onset and Rime Onset is the part of a syllable that precedes the vowel. Rime is the remainder of the syllable.

Paired Reading A method of fostering reading fluency where the beginning reader is "coached" by parent or adult to "model" their reading. A half-way stage between being read to by an adult and independent reading.

Peer Tutoring Pupils work in pairs, assisting each other in a particular area or skill. Peer tutoring is a system in which the helper as well as the child being helped benefit greatly.

Perceptuo-motor Perceptual processing difficulties which may be evident in skills such as visual motor coordination, ie handwriting,

Phoneme The smallest unit of sound in a word, eg dog has 3 phonemes: d-o–g.

Phonology The study of sounds in spoken language, how sounds are broken down into phonemes, how sounds are blended together, how to segment sounds etc.

Pragmatics The use of language; how the child uses language.

Primary Language System Language is generally seen as a code by which our thoughts and ideas are expressed through symbols, ie words. These words can be in the form of spoken words which is the Primary Language System or written words which is the Secondary Language System.

Processing A mental activity which involves the learner interacting with the material to be learned.

Receptive Language Understanding and comprehension of spoken and written language (see *Expressive Language*).

Rime The final part of the sound in a one-syllable word; onset is the beginning sound (see *Onset and Rime*).

SCAD Refers to subtests of the Wechsler Intelligence Scale for Children, ie Symbol Search, Coding, Arithmetic, Digit Span.

SERC Report of the Special Education Review Committee, 1993, Department of Education.

SLT Speech and Language Therapist. A specialist in the diagnosis and treatment of speech and language difficulties and disorders.

Secondary Language System Words which are expressed in written form (see Primary Language System).

Serial Probability The probability that certain letters will occur together in a given word or that certain letters will follow each other.

Short-term (Working) Memory A second memory storage within the information–processing model. It is a temporary storage facility serving as working memory as a problem receives one's conscious attention.

Special Needs "Extra" or "exceptional" needs which an individual may have, in addition to the common needs of all learners.

Specific Learning Disabilities/SLDs "Impairment in specific aspects of reading, writing and arithmetical notation, the primary cause of which is not attributable to assessed ability being below the average range, to defective sight or hearing, emotional factors, a physical condition or to any extrinsic adverse circumstances." (DES, SERC Report, 1993)

Speech Therapist Also known as Speech and Language Therapist in UK and Speech Pathologist in USA. A specialist in the diagnosis and treatment of speech and language difficulties and disorders.

Standardised Test Tests which have been standardised on a large population and have national norms. Such tests give a standardised score, percentile rank and other statistical information for comparison purposes.

WISC Weschler Intelligence Scale for Children, 3rd UK edition of the American test. This is the most commonly used standardised intelligence test for children aged 6 - 16.

Whole Language Approach An integrated approach to teaching reading, writing and oral language, whereby reading, writing and spelling are not seen as separate activities but integrated with oral language.

Sources for Glossary

Department of Education & Science (1999). *Primary School Curriculum – English Language and Teacher Guidelines*. Dublin: The Stationery Office.

Lerner, J. (1997). *Learning Disabilities: Theories, Diagnosis and Teaching Strategies*. Boston: Houghton Mifflin.

Ott, P. (1997). *How to Detect and Manage Dyslexia: A Reference and Resource Manual*. Oxford: Heinemann.

APPENDIX

A SAMPLE OF USEFUL TESTS FOR DIAGNOSTIC ASSESSMENT

Individual Reading Tests

Neale Analysis of Reading Ability — Second ed. Revised (1997). Ages 6 - 12.11. Windsor: NFER Nelson.

Macmillan Individual Reading Analysis. (1987). Windsor: NFER Nelson.

The Standard Reading Tests (1977). J.C. Daniels & Hunter Diack.

Individual Word Recognition Tests

Graded Word Reading Test (1985). (age 6 –14). Windsor: NFER Nelson.

Marino Graded Word Reading Scale. (1970). Séamas V. Ó Súilleabháin C.F.C. Dublin: Longman Browne and Nolan.

Test of General Ability

Non Reading Intelligence Tests/NRIT (1989). D. Young. London: Hodder & Stoughton.

Spelling Tests: Group & Individual

British Spelling Test Series 1-5. (1985). Windsor: NFER Nelson.

Diagnostic Spelling Test (1982) (age 7-11). Vincent. D., & Claydon, J. Windsor: NFER Nelson.

Schonell Graded Spelling Test (out of print).

Spelling in Context (1993). (Ages 5 –12) Peters & Smith. Windsor: NFER Nelson.

Test of Phonological Awareness

Phonological Assessment Battery (PhAB) (1997) Fredrickson, Frith, & Reason. Windsor: NFER Nelson.

Mathematics Test

Profile of Mathematical Skills (1979). France, N. Ages 8 – 14. Windsor: NFER Nelson.

Early Screening Test

Middle Infant Screening Test & Forward Together Programme (1993). Age 5-6 Hannavy. NFER Nelson.

Quest: Screening Diagnostic and Remediation Kit (2nd Ed.). (1995). Age 6-8. Robertson *et al.* Windsor: NFER-Nelson.